a million ^tiny things

a million ^tiny things

a mother's urgent search
for hope in a changing climate

kenna lee

Mole's Hill Press
Sebastopol, CA

Mole's Hill Press
Sebastopol, CA
www.moleshillpress.com

First Edition Copyright © 2012 by Kenna Lee

ISBN: 978-0-9850215-0-4

LIBRARY OF CONGRESS CATALOGING-IN-PUBLICATION DATA
Library of Congress Control Number: 2012901821
Lee, Kenna.
A Million Tiny Things

Memoir is by necessity a record of remembered events. The author
acknowledges that her memory is subjective and at times faulty, and begs
forgiveness for any mistakes contained herein.

Design by Charity Grace Kirk of Purple Persimmon
Printed in the United States of America using FSC certified paper.

www.milliontinythings.com

For Bright Eyes, Mowgli, and The Percussionist.
And, of course and always, for Cedar.

Contents

It is not a terrible thing to love the world, knowing that the world is always passing and irrecoverable, to be known only in loss. To love anything good, at any cost, is a bargain.

Wendell Berry
Jayber Crow

Mom, can you just forget about the earth for *one minute* and buy me some plastic?

Bright Eyes, age 4

prologue

There is no such thing as a free pony.

Just before our first son's first birthday, an acquaintance offered to give us a pony, a "wonderfully gentle and easy" tiny white pony that her son had outgrown. Bestill my Tennessee-bred heart! Of course my barely-toddling firstborn needed a pony. Never mind that the plot of land we inhabit in northern California, the "country-lite" suburban parcel to which we fondly refer as the "biggest acre in town," is a far cry from the 100-acre farm where I grew up. It was a pony! A free pony. And, never mind that my domestic partner is not really a horse person, and that I was nine months pregnant with our second child (my partner gave birth to our first). And having been on ponies well before I was out of diapers myself, I should have been aware that in general, ponies tend to be less "gentle and easy" than ornery and obstinate. Never mind anything—it was a free pony! Even my partner, usually the pragmatic voice of reason, got carried away by the moment.

Predictably, well before our second son turned one, the very decrepit, shaggy Freckles had become semi-affectionately known as the "thousand-dollar free pony." Adequate fencing, extensive dental work, and the massive amount of special "senior food" and ground-up, pelletized hay required to maintain a healthy if toothless nutrition status, well, it added up. And continued to add up, as the years ticked by. Now, as my story begins, the boys are four and three, little wolf-cub bellies sticking out over their elastic-band jeans as they gambol about the "field." (Well, it has a fence, grass, and a pony, so we tend to call it a field even though it is very, very small.) We have come down here for a final, late-summer blackberry gathering expedition, in hopes of stocking our freezer with some juicy treats for midwinter. For this is how I picture myself: a food-gathering and preserving, homestead-y, off-the-grid, ready for the post-carbon economy kind of mother. But there is no such idyllic I'm-such-an-earth-mother food harvest and storage happening here. Instead, I'm on my hands and knees, head bent toward the weedy ground, keenly aware that I make a comic parallel silhouette to the four-legged, grazing pony just a few feet away.

I'm unable to move from the spot where I have sunk down, and the boys are circling me, unsure what to do. "I'm alright," I manage to gasp out for the benefit of the eldest, his blue eyes widening below his sunbleached mess of curls. We've started to call him The Percussionist, due to an increasingly apparent prodigal-quality to his drumming, but underneath the banging, he's one of those sensitive boys, slowly furrowing his brow with worry about the sudden lack of verticality in his mother. Three-year-old Mowgli, in contrast, olive and brown where his brother is fair, feral to his brother's tameness, is thrilled by the new development. Mama is retching in the field: cool!

This is NOT what I planned for today. Today was supposed to be nature and wild berries and mama wolf wrestling with her cubs in the grass after a pony ride. Not paralysis brought on by overpowering, sudden nausea. Time to admit that I'm pregnant. And a bit ambivalent about having reneged on my plan to only give birth once, you know, to avoid the whole overpopulation, overconsumption, overheating the earth thing.

Before we had any kids, The Pragmatist and I approached family planning with an eye toward ecology, balanced out by biological urges. We would each give birth to just one child, and then, if we wanted to expand our family, we would adopt. But when I became pregnant, just after she gave birth to our first son, I felt an unexpected grief. I could scarcely rejoice in the excitement of the life singing within me, echoing as I was with a melancholy refrain: you'll never feel this/do this/be this again. My partner could not bear my sadness; after all the sweat and tears that had been necessary for me to get pregnant, she wanted me to enjoy it. So she opened the Pandora's box of possibility: why not just do it, have another one? Just one more child won't be the cause of wholesale environmental destruction. And from there, I have ended up here, brought to my knees by this compromise of my ideals.

So, like any other guilt-ridden wanna-be eco-mother trying to boost her green credentials, I turn to the internet for tips. Once I have dragged myself back to the house, and miraculously gotten the boys down napping, I head for one of my favorite green websites, and search "pregnancy."

Oh, yikes, I'm really pregnant. Again. And here's what I find the internet (www.ewg.org/healthyhometips/toxicfreechildren) has to say about *that*:

- Print out a list of the fruits and veggies you should always buy organic. (Check.)

- For your water, use a reverse osmosis system or carbon filter pitcher to reduce exposure to impurities such as chlorine, perchlorate and lead. Don't drink bottled water. If you're out and about, use a stainless steel, glass or BPA-free plastic reusable container. (Steel water bottle, check. Except, did I hear something about a scandal involving the linings of steel water bottles?)

- Only eat low-mercury seafood. Carry a reference list. (No sushi, check.)

- Use iodized salt: iodine buffers against chemicals such as perchlorate that can disrupt your thyroid system and pose potential risks for your baby's brain development during pregnancy. (Huh?)

- Just because the label says "gentle" or "natural" doesn't mean a product is safe for pregnancy. Read the ingredients and avoid triclosan, fragrance and oxybenzone. (On the to-do list.)

- Wash maternity clothes before wearing. Clothing is often coated with chemical treatments in the factory. (Seriously? *Maternity* clothes? Thank god for all my hand-me-downs.)

- Test your tap water for lead and avoid any home remodeling if your house was built before 1978, when lead house paint was banned. (Can't afford to remodel, hurrah!)

- Household cleaners, bug killers, pet treatments and air fresheners can contain hazardous chemicals. Check out less toxic alternatives. (Already paranoid because of the boys, check.)

- Some plastics contain toxic chemicals, including BPA and phthalates. Don't reuse single-use containers or microwave food in plastic containers. Avoid PVC by hanging a natural-fabric shower curtain. (Um, well, gotta get on that shower curtain thing. Didn't I read that IKEA has some non-toxic plastic ones? My partner, The Pragmatist, is no way going to go for another hemp curtain after that incident with the mildew.)

- Avoid gasoline fumes. Ask for your partner's help to fill the gas tank, or use full service. (Oh, get real. As if. Does full service even exist outside of Oregon & New Jersey?)

Let me sum this up: everything is toxic, don't go anywhere or buy anything, grow your own food and stop cleaning the house. And don't drink the water. No problem, since I mostly can't get more than a few yards from the bathroom before I have to head back for just one more episode of retching, and any water intake immediately sets off a new round. I'll just stay home with a case of ginger ale.

While, my head is spending a lot of time in the toilet bowl, The Percussionist prowls nervously and Mowgli dances his excitement around the bathroom asking, over and over, "Can

I flush?!?" I guess this is a good time to be grateful that The Pragmatist hasn't yet agreed to convert to composting toilets.

———————

Needless to say, there wasn't any extra energy during that period to write a book. I was spending all my time trying to walk the tightrope of sustainability: living as green as possible while still living. Just making it hour to hour, trying to eat something with a small amount of nutritional value. Getting crazier and crazier as I saw the demands of two children plus pregnancy, then two children plus baby, sucking (literally, on the part of the baby) my resources dry just at the moment of my life when I was overcome with a passion for preserving a safe and livable world for them. Second-guessing every decision, and trying to stay vertical as often as I could.

The book came later, once I had returned to work. One day as I pulled my lunch from the fridge in our office kitchen, I noticed two different "save the planet—it's easy" magnets stuck to the freezer door right at eye level. "10 Ways You Can Help Stop Global Warming" listed recycling, driving less, all the usuals, including "replace appliances with energy efficient models." "Live Green" covered the same territory until it suddenly, strikingly disagreed. "Don't replace appliances until they wear out," it argued. And the race was on, in my mind at least. Wait a friggin minute! Don't these people talk to each other? Can't they get on the same page? No wonder I was so tortured by the million tiny decisions I made daily, much smaller than appliances, but far greater in number.

I felt like I spent an unreasonable amount of energy trying to figure out which of all the "try this to green your life" suggestions were most important, and which were, given my often stretched-thin-trying-to-meet-the-basic-needs-of-three-kids-and-a-partner life, realistic and doable. And blaming myself whenever "realistic and doable" fell short of perfect. I was definitely past anxious and heading straight for plain old neurotic.

In the past, whenever I felt overwhelmed and neurotic and heading into an endless downward spiral, I would read Anne Lamott's book of essays *Traveling Mercies*, and I would snap out of it. Because here's someone even more neurotic, even more overwhelmed, overall just crazier than me, and somehow she manages to learn to forgive herself and live anyway. And sure, she does it with the help of her buddy Jesus, but still, she does it. So maybe there's hope for me, even though Jesus is more of a childhood acquaintance I've fallen out of touch with, someone I'm expecting a Facebook friend request from any day now. But *Traveling Mercies* wasn't working this time, because my anxieties had become more specific, entirely focused on the environment. I needed another book, but I couldn't find it. I found a million saying I could make my life better if I made it greener, but I couldn't find anything that allowed me to forgive myself for continuing to destroy the planet on which my children are doomed to live. (Hmm. I wonder why?) I began jotting notes, writing essays in stolen early-morning hours, to feel less alone. The essays started to pile up, get published. Maybe I wasn't so alone.

Just at that moment, the hospice where I work began a TWR, pronounced "twer." Temporary Work Reduction. Ours went on so long that the word "temporary" seemed like a bad joke, but despite the concomitant reduction in income, there were some fringe benefits. Like, since it's "temporary," and thus apt to end at any time, it seems like a good idea not to let go of the toddler-whispering babysitter on Wednesday mornings, nor to mess with the Fridays-with-the-other-mom schedule we created when I regularly worked on Fridays. Yep, that would be one child-free morning PLUS all day Fridays, an embarrassment of riches. And sure, a lot of that time got taken up in blissfully unencumbered trips to the grocery store, bank, video store, you name it, but there was still time left over to sit at the teahouse with my laptop and get enough of a book written that once I did start working again, there was no going back, even if that meant drinking way too much previously-forsworn coffee and staying up way too late at night, propped up in bed with the computer sliding off my lap just before my chin hit my chest.

So, yeah, I wanted a book and, not finding it on the shelf, I wrote it, doing my best to describe how I really lived it. You'll notice that in the first year post-baby, true-to-life, there are entire months missing. May, um, haze. November, probably a turkey in there. December, some sort of Santa-related frenzy. But seriously, every mom I know misses entire months of her kid's first year, and after number three, my memory has become, shall we say, "porous" at best. (Plain old "poor" might be more accurate.) But I've done my best to capture what it was like to live through the long days of small-child parenting, when I over and over tried and failed and succeeded, sometimes all in the same day and not always in that order, to make my peace with living a modern life with three children on a fragile planet.

I know that the very fact of having written a book destroys my credibility as an overworked, overstressed, too-busy mom. I never could understand all those essays and books where a mother bemoans her hectic life and describes how hard it is to get anything done. "You wrote an essay/article/book, you freak," I'd always think to myself. "You must have had a little free time. Stop whining." So you can take the whining with a grain of salt, but do yourself a favor, and take the forgiveness with a spoonful of honey. Because I'm almost definitely even more neurotic, even more overwhelmed, overall just crazier than you, and somehow I do manage to learn to forgive myself and live anyway.

year one

Here in the Marais we wake early in the mornings and are in bed early at night. We miss National Public Radio. We miss recycling, as silly and meager as that sounds. Everything we use here must be thrown away, and it bothers us, robbed of our rituals of composting and reclamation, our daily treks out back to the rot-heap, where we offer the Earth scraps of itself, returning nature to nature! Expediting the Global Easter, when all shall rise again! Though we mean it, and mean to, we've never actually used the compost: it is merely an act of apology.

Lorrie Moore
Who Will Run the Frog Hospital?

april

The elements of high drama are all there: the sun fading between towering redwood trunks, a woman's desperate scream escaping from a bedroom window, dust billowing as tires rush to ascend a gravel drive. But the person who jumps from the car is not a police officer, handgun ready for a confrontation, but simply a hurrying midwife, arms laden with bags of medical equipment and herbs, an oxygen tank slung over her shoulder. She pushes open my front door with her hip. I'm the woman in the bedroom, wailing my daughter into the welcoming air.

The birth of any child ranks as a life-changing day, replete with the profound emotions that accompany the glimpsed transition between worlds, the transformation of the imagined into the real. But this time there is none of the heightened anxiety of a first birth, nor are there any life-threatening complications leading to obvious spiritual insights. After all, this is our third child, the second to whom I have given birth, and she comes out with relatively little fanfare (if quite a bit of noise on my part). What makes the day of her birth so momentous is this: it's the day I have to admit that I'm just like everybody else.

Here's my confession: I've spent my life being, um, shall we say, just a tad bit self-righteous. Everybody has his soapbox issue, and the environment has long been mine. I was green way before it became the new black. I had an apoplectic fit in the early 90's when I discovered that UNICEF's holiday cards weren't printed on recycled paper. "Don't they *get it?*" I savagely griped from between clenched teeth. "Don't they get that they can't claim to be saving children if they are destroying virgin forests to print cards, the same virgin forests that are preserving the biodiversity and even the *oxygen* (for godsake) that will enable those children to live as adults in a healthy world? What are they thinking?!?"

UNICEF was by no means the only target of my scorn. Corporations, consumers, politicians, voters, just about everyone got the same comments: Don't they get it? What are they thinking? I sat atop my pile of recyclables, carefully tearing the plastic windows out of junk mail envelopes so I would not contaminate the paper recycling process, and judging.

Admit it, you've done it too, even if you've tried not to—that old Judgment just snuck in through the back door when you were looking the other way. Well, before my daughter was born, Judgment wasn't lurking around the back, he was sitting right at home up on the front porch, just a-swaying and a-rocking in the old porch swing. Creak, creak, creak, sounded the chains as they measured his slow arc. I'd bring him a glass of homemade organic lemonade and whisper gossip in his ear, "Can you *believe* that the neighbors over there are spending so much on that big addition and *they don't even have solar panels?* They say they can't afford them, hah. Don't they get it?" Then

I'd turn to face the other way and point a few doors down. "And those folks. What are *they* thinking, getting dirt bikes for their kids, training the next generation in the recreational destruction of the planet through wanton use of fossil fuels?" Judgment would sit there, picking the peeling paint from the armrest on the swing, grinning and nodding between sips.

Back then, when I only had two kids, a friend came up from the city one day to visit our semi-rural acre of Northern California paradise, bringing her daughter in their sparkling new silver minivan. When we decided to head into town for ice cream, we all piled into the van, three adults and three kids, with room to spare. Compared to our fuel-efficient mini-wagon, it felt like pure luxury, like sitting in a comfortable living room instead of a car. "Oh, this is so nice," I offered the compliment to our carpool hostess, but not without a backhanded holier-than-thou swipe, "too bad for us, I just can't reconcile my conscience with the gas mileage." The poor Pragmatist flinched, embarrassed by my deplorable manners.

Fast forward a few months, and there I was, sweating out the details on the showroom floor, as I traded in the cramped wagon for a den-sized minivan. Leaning over my awkward pooch of a second-trimester belly to sign my name to the deal: trading thirty mpg for twenty, downgrading my personal mpg by a third, the perfect inverse to the upgrade to my offspring by a third. I heard a sermon about that time, in which the preacher prayed: "may you do the thing you most judge," and I'll confess, it's a real life-changer. Takes you down a few pegs, right off the top of the recycling heap into a more compassionate and forgiving arena.

The ecological compromises we would make because of this third child, the burden that is placed on our planet by global population growth, the unfairly large consumption of limited resources by each American—these were things we understood. Which was the whole reason we had decided to limit ourselves to two in the first place. Two was a somewhat arbitrary number—why not one, or none? Or eight, since I used to work among Amish families, whose eight or ten children live more lightly on the earth than any two of mine do. But two made sense to us, and two was our limit. This was an entirely rational, values-based decision, the kind that should be easy to stick to, right?

Um, right, until that moment when I ceased to be rational, when my unadulterated gut-driven desire became stronger than my values. I wanted number three more than I wanted to feel good about my choices. I wanted her that much, so I had her. And now with her, I will have less time and energy for staying on the straight and narrow green path, more processed frozen meals, and of course, the low-mpg minivan.

Of course, I won't stop trying—I'll wash my own cloth diapers in my high-efficiency, low-water washing machine, feeling righteous as I bypass the stacks of disposable diapers in the supermarket. But soon, as I research further righteous action on the internet, I will get bitch-slapped by a quote from someone at a place called the Sustainability Institute, undercutting my sense of cloth-diapered accomplishment: "It's great to try to move our lives in the direction of ecological righteousness, but it's also true that every human activity has environmental impact – – especially the activities of that fraction of the human population rich enough to have diapers of any kind. From the earth's point of view it's not all that important which kind of diapers you use. The important decision was having the baby." Shit, I'll sigh. What was I thinking? Don't I, of all people, get it?

Well sure, I do get it, most of the time; but this time, thinking was not what I was doing. I was indulging a deep desire, the same way the people across the road desired a sense of comfort in their master bedroom, the same way the neighbors down the street wanted a motorbike track to keep their almost-teenage kids relatively safe in their own back yard for another year or two. Maybe we all get it. Maybe our better selves are all whispering pro-environment slogans softly into our ears, but the idea that we each have to save the whole planet just feels too overwhelming, too amorphous, and so much less immediate than our human-felt thrumming desires.

I'll probably have some moments of third-child regret, when I venture out to gas up the minivan and see a mom buckling her two kids into twin carseats stashed neatly in the back of a Prius. But now, looking into the still wet-cheesy face, into her dark sparking eyes, life without my number three, without this bright-eyed daughter, is simply unimaginable. Life without her would not be my life. In days to come I may sometimes wish our carseats could all fit into a Prius, and even feel guilty for having had her, but in this liminal newborn state I understand that when that happens, there will be a reprieve: Bright Eyes will turn her too-big head to face me, her broken-wide gummy grin will crack open my clinched-tight heart, and I will start to forgive myself. And in that grateful moment of generosity, I will start to forgive everyone else, too.

Of course, my back door will stay cracked open and my old friend will sneak in more than I'd like him to. But from now on I'll try to keep him in the kitchen. I'll just tell him,

"You hush up, Judgment. Drink your lemonade, and then let yourself out. I've got laundry to do."

june

On the bright yellow day when my daughter turns seven weeks old, I suddenly realize, oh my god, this is it, this is my life now. I get out of bed each morning, fix breakfast for myself and the boys, spend a blur of hours caring for all three kids while The Pragmatist works. The foggy post-partum period is over: I am no longer officially recovering, though I won't return to my own part-time job for a few more weeks. The big event of the birth has been told and retold, now more a memory of the telling than of the day itself. The horrifying ambivalence of the pregnancy has been forced to recede by the immutable fact of my daughter's physical presence in our lives. Bright Eyes kicks her blanket off, and there she is, her own smooth, pink self. I step back and look at her lying in the middle of the changing table, with its hand-me-down chipped goldenrod paint, and it is as if I am seeing her for the first time.

You see, beyond the endless stream of diaper changes, there's this whole, larger than life, mothering-a-girl thing. Suddenly, looking at her undeniably female body, the small cleft between her soft pads of labia, the tiny tonguetip of clitoris peeking shyly out, I feel an intense urgency to heal all my old gender-related wounds so that I can walk my daughter into womanhood intact and unscarred. But the wounds inflicted by growing up female in a culture directed by the male gaze are deep, and I'm spending most of my energy just trying to get healthy food on the table and wash the diapers. I tell her she's pretty, and I tell her she's strong and smart and capable, and I hope that for the moment that's enough. I worry that with my own scars incompletely healed, I'm not up to the task of mothering a woman-to-be.

Trying to stay "in the moment" (that's what we do here in Northern Cal), I stare down at Bright Eyes' still-fresh pink body on the changing table. As I lift her legs to slide the clean folded diaper underneath, I notice that she is rapidly growing into herself. She has what can only be described as a real butt, where less than two months ago there were just two flesh-covered bony bumps. She fills my hands more each day, and looking out the window at my tree-scaling boys, I see how quickly she will outgrow my grasp altogether. As I'm spackling white paste onto her slightly rashy bottom, she kicks hard, and I have a moment of surprise that she can still wiggle, so alive, underneath the heavy blankets of fear and expectation I have piled on top of her. Looking at her tiny vagina and clitoris fills me with a vague but pressing terror. My raw desire for her to survive intact, to find the rightness of her own physical self, paralyzes me with fear.

In talking to other mothers of girls, I have discovered that my fears about raising a daughter in a world that still both over-glorifies and over-sanctions the female body are actually, sadly, normal anxieties: small-girl-in-the-big-bad-world general worries. But eco-obsessed as I am, I also have some very specific worries: about two million of them, nestled right here inside her tiny, palm-sized abdomen. Her eggs, already all there, already vulnerable to assault from toxic chemicals and heavy metals, radiation and electromagnetic fields. All there will ever be, already here. Talk about upping the ante.

For now, I not only need to reach some feminist enlightenment of personal healing to mother my daughter, I have to heal an entire world. A world steeped in pollution, and greed, and ever-rising carbon levels.

Any worry I might have already had about toxic exposures in my home has suddenly increased by an order of magnitude. These worries are constantly multiplied by the news broadcast on the radio, blaring in the headlines, and flashing in the ads on the side of whatever website I'm visiting: "New study shows…" it always starts, and then tells me that one more form of paint/plastic/bedding/household cleaner is *verboten*, poison to my daughter and her tiny little potential offspring. Any breathing room I might have thought I had, just because we were a household of "green" products, has disappeared. There I am on the internet late at night, typing long lists of ingredients from the side of our "all-natural" shampoo bottle into the toxin-search field on my favorite eco-website. Just in case.

I have the unfortunate memory of attending a lecture several years ago in which a fertility specialist explained that even if a woman quit smoking a long time previously, residue remains in her ovaries, giving her former habit away, little tiny toxins clinging to her future children. Oh, plus, apparently dormant eggs can't perform the normal cellular repair processes. So, I am convinced that the viability of the next generation of my family depends entirely on my ability to create a tiny toxin-free bubble within a polluted world, preserving the pristine fluids in which my daughter's oocytes rest, awaiting their chance to become my grandchildren. I upgrade from merely hormone-free Ben & Jerry's to 100% organic, locally produced by righteous farmers (and commensurately priced) ice cream for my pint-a-day breastfeeding diet. Because she's worth it.

With the future grandkids' DNA in mind, I unplug the wireless router in our house, creating all sorts of inconvenience, but someone told me that the wireless signals aren't good for kids, and I'm obsessed with the "precautionary principle," by which new technologies should be assumed potentially harmful until proven otherwise. I conveniently forget to apply this principle to the cordless phone or the cell phone, until one of the local townsfolk makes national headlines by fighting successfully to prevent our town from installing social-justice inspired free wireless service, on the grounds that the electro-magnetic fields are too dangerous. She says that my cordless and cell phones are just as bad, and I shouldn't let the kids use them. I immediately go online and order an old-fashioned, refurbished corded phone, but it sits in a box under my desk, because I can't manage to both care for the baby and install the jack that will make the phone's location convenient enough that we'll actually use it. I make sure that at least the cordless is on speaker mode when the boys talk to their grandparents so it won't be so close to their little growing brains.

But mostly, I worry. Because I'm overwhelmed with getting the diapers clean and getting the food bought and on the table. And soon, I'll be back at work, driving around all day by burning a poison-creating, non-renewable resource. I'm living in this world that I don't know how to fix, and I want to just have the same work my mother had in raising her three kids: give them love, and healthy food, and some basic values. That seems like more than enough to manage with two preschoolers and a new baby. But it's not enough, and I can't really ever forget it. Still, I can't not do those things because I'm out trying to fix the planet. So for now, I buy organic, I wash our third-time around diapers, and I focus on my daughter's still-forming face, looking there for both the hope and stamina I will need.

And if, as I contemplate her physicality, snapping the diaper around her little egg-carrying belly, what I see is my own recycled fear, this is what I do: I force my eyes to linger, to keep looking through the pangs of my own reflection in her face. She is not me, will not be me, and I remind myself not to reduce her by making assumptions about her unlived life based on my own. She will have her own wounds and her own healings, her own journeys and her own future, of which I may know only a little. But there will be one person whose eyes can be steady, even if my steps aren't always sure. This is my decision: I will wipe the worry out of my face, and I will look at my daughter's dark shimmering eyes. I will look past my reflection until I see her, and then I will hold her in my own powerful gaze, beautiful and whole.

I snug the Velcro diaper cover around her thighs, fasten it tight, and then, for just this moment, I let go of the angst associated with raising a woman in this so-called post-feminist, toxic world. I let go of my struggle against both genderized generalizations and our carbon-spewing culture, and for just this moment, I revel in her, in her vulnerable, egg-carrying girl-ness. She gazes up, following my movements with bright-eyed wonder, waving her milk-padded calves at me. I reach down for her half-naked puppy body, pull her up into the cradle of my neck, and nuzzle her, murmuring gleefully, "Who's got the girl? Who's got the girl?"

"I've got the girl. Mama's got her powerful and strong, free-range, beautiful baby girl."

july

The heat of summer has descended upon our town, sending us all to the concrete lawn extending out to one side of the public pool. Chubby-faced Bright Eyes sticks to my half-exposed breast, her milky drool mixing with the rivulets of sweat running down under the bikini top I'm wearing to show off my still-postpartum cleavage. This temporary endowment of detectable breasts to the chronically flat-chested is one of the few enjoyable physiological effects of childbirth. Of course, after the boobs comes the sagging, so "carpe diem!" my C-cup bikini top shouts.

It is a small miracle that we are here at all, on time, all four of us in pool-appropriate clothing (which for one of us means an oft-misplaced reusable swim diaper) and with a workable number of towels. All hail to the mothers of infants who manage to get out of the house, I say. Never mind that the sun hats are still sitting at home in the front hall, and our sunblock application is rather smeary.

The Percussionist and Mowgli sit several yards away dangling their feet into the water, sullen conspirators in swim lesson noncooperation. Every other kid I know is industriously blowing bubbles, or splashing a kickboard down a swim lane, or at least chanting "motorboat, motorboat, go so fast," a game which ends with a perfunctory wetting of the head. My normally irrepressible boys, like a pair of demure southern belles worried about their hairdos, remain completely dry from the waist up. When the teenaged teacher gives up trying to coax them into the water, I flipflop over to do some cajoling of my own.

"Remember, how once you guys learn to swim, we're going to go canoeing?" I start, squatting down on sweat-slick thighs beside them. "You don't have to put your heads under, just at least hold onto the edge and kick, okay? Please." No luck for me, the only grown-up within several feet of the pool, my kids and I the center of attention for the peanut gallery of waiting parents, whom I imagine to be starting to take bets on my chances of success. "C'mon guys. If you'll get in and kick, we can get bagels for lunch." No go. "And a smoothie, all you have to do is get in," I up the ante, and it looks like I might have a taker.

"A superfood smoothie, mom?" asks Mowgli, ever one to perform for sugar, even sugar with "green micronutrients" added.

"Yes, a superfood smoothie, and bagels."

"Hooray!" he and his brother both look cheered by this offer of their favorite treat lunch.

"But you have to get in," I remind them. "Before the class is over."

Silence. Inaction. More silence, as the gleefully soggy children in front of us crow their damn "motorboat, motorboat" song at higher and higher pitches.

"Looks like class is almost over guys. Last chance." Last chance for me to not have the only kids in the whole town who won't get wet during swim lessons. As the minutes tick down, lame parenting technique #1, bribery, gives way to lame parenting technique #2, threats. "I guess we can't have any ice cream today, since you won't get in," and so forth. Public poolside parenting at its bleakest, the other parents all either politely pretending to look away or hurling their pitying, compassionate glances toward me. And I'm not really sure if they're judging me, or if I'm judging myself. Usually, when I see another mom struggling with recalcitrant preschoolers, I think simply "there but for the grace of god (or whoever you believe in) go I." In rational moments, I assume that most other parents think the same. But balancing the baby on one thigh here at the edge of the pool, sighing as the end-of-lesson whistle blows, I know *someone* is judging, even if I'm not sure who. Judgment is definitely hanging around, sending my thoughts careening well-past the immediate moment toward greater failures than this one.

Maybe it's that my imagination is held captive by an entire childhood of Sunday mornings spent in linoleum-floored, fluorescent-lit rooms with construction paper cutout arks plastering eggshell-painted drywall, well-meaning matrons reading from an illustrated book of Bible stories. But I like to think that it probably has more to do with the recurring template of editorial page cartoons: loopy black lines across the bottom of the frame, a cloudbank floor upon which perches a podium. Behind the podium, the parabolic downcurve of a barred gate swoops from misty towers of yet more clouds. Just two characters comprise the scene—a bushily white-bearded, berobed gentleman consults a ledger, while a supplicant beseeches him with tensely raised shoulders and desperate eyes. The punchline changes from year to year, but the basic set-up remains stable: judgment day.

Technically, I don't believe in judgment day. I certainly don't believe that some man standing in the sky will tally me up into black and red columns and come up with a final number that determines my eternity. I don't even really believe in 'karma' the way it is generally understood by the people I hear using the word, that what-goes-around-comes-around. The way I see it, if bad people were always punished for bad acts, we wouldn't need a criminal justice system. If good people were always rewarded for good acts, we'd all be out there dumping our wallets into the outstretched palms of the homeless man on the shoulder of the offramp, instead of averting our eyes and pulling our cars forward, craning our necks into oncoming traffic to move quickly past the question he asks us: are you kind, or stingy, or pretending to yourself that you gave at the office? His question lingers, despite my agnostic approach to the justice of fate, as if underneath what I think I believe there lurks Saint Peter, or perhaps just Santa, ticking off the columns, and asking each time: good or bad, which are you?

I know I'm asking myself this question a lot these days. Am I good because I don't hit my kids when I'm at the end of my rope, or bad because I growl viciously at them from between clenched teeth? Good for buying produce from a local farm, or bad for succumbing to the temptation of shipped-from-Mexico bananas? Good for carpooling, or bad for driving a 19-mpg minivan in the first place? Good for being aware of the environmental impacts of my decisions, or bad for continuing to live within the template of an unsustainable culture?

In the ledger of my self-esteem, the 'bad' column gets the most ink. I try to give myself credit for what I'm doing right, but the value of my stumbling stepwise efforts breaks down when I look at Bright Eyes. I think about all her little eggs, and then I think about her children and the world they will inherit from me. I can see their questioning eyes settling onto myself, by then white-haired and obstinate, distilled into my purest form by time. They are wondering why we didn't do more. In this scenario, the difficulty I have now in avoiding plastics, overly processed foods, and made-in-China non-essentials seems an indulgence, pure luxury, almost a bad joke—the irrationality of human behavior seen through the telescopic lens of hindsight, forty years of climate change from now.

So I guess I do believe in judgment day, that day in the unseen future when I will have to look at my grandchildren and justify the choices I'm making today. I can already hear my excuses, my rationalizations, my attempts to explain to them how it all seemed kind of unreal, how we all thought that someone else was responsible, that some government scientist would fix it, that recycling and biofuels would be enough. They will not understand. They will point to the history books which tell them that all the information was available to us for so long, and so widely broadcast. They will tilt their curious heads and with heartbreaking innocence hang the word heavily on my guilty conscience: why? Why couldn't you see? Why didn't you act?

There are many answers to their questions. Denial, laziness, denial, inertia, and denial being a few. But there's also the fact that in the now, without the clarity of hindsight, the proper course of action doesn't always seem clear. Within a changing world, how do we know what is good and what is bad? Case in point: what should I do with my tax refund, put it aside in the solar panels fund or add it to the kids' college savings? Will my kids need more education to prosper in a rapidly mutating culture (college fund), or does book-learning matter less on a frying planet (solar panels)? And shouldn't I place the needs of everyone (solar panels) ahead of the needs of a few (college fund)? But won't everyone need well-educated leaders to help through the transition (college fund)? Do we triage the immediate crisis of carbon emissions (solar panels) as more urgent than the potentially drug/alcohol/sex-wasted four years of the undergraduate experience? Where is the compass pointing toward "right?"

I have a great desire to be able to look into my grandchild's face and say: we tried. We did what we could. We did our best. But I'm not sure I'll be able to. This very morning I took a hot shower, quickly washed my hair and body, and then stood under the steaming stream of water—water pumped out of the ground by electricity and heated by burning natural gas. I stood there, the hot cascade pouring into my stiff shoulders, waiting for the ratio of pleasure to guilt to reach a tipping point which would make me crank the valves closed. I turned them off sooner than I wanted to, later than I should have.

The Pragmatist insists, "You do a lot. Cut yourself some slack." But I'm not so sure that I really do "a lot." More than many, less than some; either way, probably not enough from my grandchildren's perspective. How much is enough, and how do we know? I am haunted by one of the closing scenes in "Schindler's List," where Oscar Schindler looks at his car, his ring, all the things he kept, and regrets aloud how many more lives he could have saved had he given those things up. I ask myself, in what ways could I do more, sacrifice more? In what ways could I probably do more without even really sacrificing anything of importance to me? How much more would I have to do to get on the "good" list?

I have no conclusion. I am living in this swamp of questions, searching for solid ground where my feet can rest, exhausted from kicking to keep my mouth above the murky surface. But when I reach my toes down, they simply encounter more slimy mud, sucking me down, down to where I'm afraid I won't be able to breathe. I stay up by wriggling a constant compromise: put half the money into a socially and environmentally screened mutual fund for the future, half into savings for the solar upgrade. And in this way I keep my thoughts swimming, my head just out of the muck, as I search for dry land, or at least water clear enough for me to know whether I am good, or bad, or pretending that what I'm doing is enough. I keep treading water in hopes that the bright sun overhead will suddenly flash on a newly posted sign, marking "this way" toward righteousness.

In the meantime, the cruel hot half hour of swim lessons is over, and I'll sit ungracefully down with my legs dangling next to the boys' in the water, just for a few seconds before I take the tiny leap from the edge down into this shallowest of possible ends, and I pause a moment to be thankful for the boys' beyond-their-tender-years heights which will allow them to stand here with their heads well above the lapping water. (I swear I don't give them hormone-laden milk; it must be something in our well water.) Balancing Bright Eyes on one sticky arm, I use the other to slide first The Percussionist, then Mowgli into the pool, both now suddenly eager to be wet. Keeping an eye out for big kid splashes that might upset the fragile but happy equilibrium of my little ledge-gripping crew, I let myself sink down until most of me, everything below the level of my nipples—where of course Bright Eyes' now-slumbering mouth still rests—feels the cool embrace of relief in this solar-heated, salty, low-chlorine sparkling water, giving me something I can finally feel good about, at least for a moment.

august

When Bright Eyes is still just a tiny little thing, but well-attached to her other mom and to her bottle of pumped milk, I head off to contribute to the financial well-being of the family. Which means I get in my car. (No, not the gas-thirsty minivan, thank goodness. For work I use our "little car," a cockroach-sized Civic that only sips the evil stuff.) As a hospice nurse, I drive from house to house, all over the back roads of my semi-rural part of the county. Then I drive home, usually stopping for an errand or two on the way.

I listen to the radio as I drive, and the radio tells me all sorts of things I don't want to know. Like the fact that each member of my typical American family consumes the same amount of the earth's resources as 32 Kenyans. By simple multiplication, the five of us are the consumption equivalent of 160 Kenyans. I neurotically search out a personal moral imperative in this arithmetic: if I had not insisted on having a third child, we would only use up as much stuff as 128 Kenyans. To make up for the indulgence of the third child, I have to reduce our overall consumption by one fifth; because we are five now instead of four, we should each consume only as much as 25.6 Kenyans. And that's just to bring us as far along in the move to reduce over-consumption as an average 4-person American family, which is to say not very far.

I drive along, heading toward home, and though the newscast has moved on to something else entirely, I'm still obsessing on the Kenyans, and what it would take to get down to only 16 Kenyan consumers each, or 5 Kenyans, or even one Kenyan, and how maybe we should move our kids to a less-developed part of the world so we could live more lightly on the earth, and how there's no reason we should have to move, we could just make different choices while living where we are. And then I pull into the only open parking space within sight of the entrance to Big Red Bullseye Megastore.

Big Red Bullseye is my downfall, in so many ways. I can go in and not get a cart or even a basket because I only need ONE THING and I know exactly what it is and I have a plan: I'll walk right to it and pick it up and walk straight back and pay and leave. From the parking lot, I hit a purposeful stride past the red concrete orbs protecting the bank of doors, but the electric door opener is one beat behind my quick pace, so I'm off-balance before I even get past the entry. As the second door swooshes closed behind me, I pause to regain my purpose, instantly lost in this vast sterile cavern over-full of bright stalactite signs and red-shirted "team members" probably making minimum wage. The big box hermetic world feels strangely pressurized, like an airplane cabin—the kind of air you don't want to breathe in too deeply, smelling of industrial cleansers and off-gassing plastics with an overlay of Starbucks.

"Surgical strike," I remind myself, re-focusing. But either the fluorescent lighting has an intentionally disorienting effect or I'm as susceptible to the passive marketing of the Big Red Bullseye floor plan as the next guy, because before I'm ten steps in, I'm *just taking a second* to browse the $1 section, remembering those half-size hammers I got for the boys back in 2004 and hoping for a similarly rare but useful find. And then I'm picking things up from those $1 bins and having to sternly lecture myself about the problems of over-consumption and cheap labor and transoceanic transport of basically junk ("but it's only *one dollar*" the devil on my left shoulder chants). And my hands only reluctantly put the aforementioned junk back in the bins and move on. I may have made it past the initial hurdle of the $1 section, but I'm not getting out any time soon. My strikes on Big Red Bullseye are about as surgical as the quagmire in Afghanistan.

I've got to go to the section where they keep the big plastic storage bins because I need a container to store some nursing supplies, and the container has to be plastic so it can stand up to regular chemical disinfection. That's all I need. One thing. Plastic bin. Eyes on the prize, sister. But if I walk straight toward my destination it means a diagonal cut through children's wear, and aren't those embroidered jeans cute, poor little Bright Eyes with all those unisex hand-me-downs from her big brothers. "NO!" shouts the tiny hemp-robed angel into my right ear. "Oppressed sweatshop workers! Eyes forward. Plastic bin. Plastic bin. One thing, remember."

I cut back to the aisle to get further away from the girl clothes, but my eyes can't resist the temptation to scan boyswear

for some essential item that will magically improve my sons'
quality of life and LOOK! Long sleeve swim shirts! Little cool-
dude surfer shirts, SPF 50, which is way higher than the low-
chemical sunblock we've been using. I pick up one in each of
the boys' sizes and then freeze beside the rack, immobilized by
the voices on either side of my head debating back and forth.

"Sweatshops. Put them back."

"Skin cancer. Buy them."

"Synthetic plastic fibers."

"Sunblock chemicals."

"Landfills full of plastics."

"Contaminated groundwater from chemical lotions"

"Birth defects in children born near the plants which
manufacture components of plastics."

"Your child bald and sickly from the chemo needed to treat
malignant melanoma."

And so on, their rhetoric getting more and more overblown
until I call a halt to it: "*enough already!*" The endgame is known,
the debate simply an indulgence of my neuroses—I will buy
the shirts, whether because there is some sort of subliminal
"consume" message coming over the canned music or because
the shorter-sighted protection of my own family keeps
trumping protection of anyone else or the planet. For the rest
of the summer, my boys will be protected from harmful UV
rays as they continue their slow dog-paddle toward becoming
safe swimmers.

And I haven't even gotten to the home storage section. Eyes
front, the slippery swimshirts in my hands are saying, you've
had your diversion, you've got more than you came for, now
you can get the bin and go home. Okay, fine, my signage-
addled brain obeys, until… look, right across from storage,

roman shades! The Pragmatist is looking for blinds for her new many-windowed studio, but her method of looking consists mainly of saying about once a week that she needs to go to Home Depot and then sighing a deep sigh. I could pick up some samples and maybe she'd like one and then won't I get major good-wife points? Oh, and the bin I came for, the bin is right here too, and now I can begin the trek back toward the checkout area.

The long plastic roman shade boxes under my arm prevent my stopping for too long in the photo album aisle, as they keep slipping and requiring an awkward readjustment. I pause by the turnoff for personal care, knowing that we must need band-aids or dental floss or q-tips but unsure which, and then I triumphantly pass the bagged candy without even a flinch, in the home stretch now. I succumb to the last minute strategic placement of nine-volt batteries (well, the battery in the smoke detector needs replacement, a valid purchase, even if unplanned, just ask my local volunteer firefighters), and with a mixture of guilt and relief I shrug the load in my arms onto one of the twenty identical red checkout counters.

The credit card machine at Big Red Bullseye always gives me a frisson of unsettledness, asking me to sign my agreement to pay for everything before the redshirt has scanned it all, but in the interest of efficiency I sign anyway; I've already signed away my intentions and integrity, why not my bank account too? I make a last-ditch attempt to salvage my anti-consumerist, environmentalist conscience by refusing to accept the red bullseye plastic bag which would make the short trip to the car so much more graceful. But I can carry it all, didn't I carry it all to the checkout? Wasn't that the whole point of not using a basket, so that my failure to resist temptation would be limited by the length of my arms if nothing else?

Disheveled and disillusioned, I trudge back to my little car, trying to feel better about my choices by comparing the fuel efficiency of my Civic to all these SUVs, by telling myself that it could have been worse. Next time, my little green angel rattles her saber, next time, we will triumph over temptation. But the little devil quietly grins, knowing that when I come back next week to return the roman shades The Pragmatist will reject, I'll have remembered that it's q-tips we need, and I'll venture just as far as the personal care aisle. From there who knows what siren song I will hear, drawing me toward some overly-packaged, eco-destructive product I don't really need? But I can at least take some meager consolation and a tiny bit of hope from the surety of this: that by now, I always know better than to get a cart.

october – january

On days when things are slow at work, my supervisor cuts me early, and then I have a window of relative freedom before The Pragmatist *et al* expect me home. This is how, in a rare, glorious moment of grocery shopping without my kids, I manage to call my friend Susan to chat. Our disparate settings magnify the distance between us: for me, it's a boiling hot October day from which I have sought refuge in an air-conditioned but frantic Discount Organics; my friend is sipping tea at home with her napping son, enjoying the breeze of arriving fall through her Brooklyn apartment windows.

But from our varied perspectives, we are both looking out at the same view: doom and gloom. That particular doom and gloom that you can't look at straight, for fear that the darkness will suck you in, or turn you to stone. Like the gaze of the medusa, it's simply too horrible to meet head on. We are friends for a reason, something within us resonates through the years and miles, and we realize this anew when we talk about our young children and the specter of weather-related apocalypse.

"I feel like I need a therapist who is a climatologist, whom I meet every week and who talks me down by reassuring me that if we just meet the carbon-reduction goals by 2020, we can still ensure a habitable planet," she explains as I round the corner of the snack aisle.

"Exactly! But, um, then don't you feel like you've turned into Andie McDowell in 'Sex, Lies, and Videotape'?" I ask, digging through the bags of dried cranberries, looking for one labeled "organic."

"Oh my God, I can't believe you just said that." Susan has been asking around, and apparently, we are the only two people she knows who still remember the opening scene of that film, in which Andie McDowell's character lies on her therapist's couch fretting about all the garbage, where it goes and how much of it there is, and (within the logic of the film, at least) totally overlooking her own issues: an unhappy marriage and familial betrayal. So, is my obsession with the changing climate just a psychological dodge from my own unconscious self and the tensions within my own domestic world? Or is it a completely sane response to the biggest challenge our species has ever created?

I triumphantly toss a bag of pesticide-free cranberries into the cart and head on toward nuts, weighing the pocketbook price of organic domestic almonds against the ecological costs of the much more popular imported non-organic cashews, all the while chattering into my (according to my neighbor) hazardously radioactive cell phone.

———

Several weeks later, I'm again noticing my kinship with Andie McDowell's trash-obsessed character, as I find myself standing in, literally, a room full of garbage. Christmas was a week ago, but we went out of town on the 26th and have just returned to our holiday-wrecked house. The "office," otherwise known as the room where everything not in use gets stashed, is wall-to-wall with empty shipping boxes half-filled with styrofoam peanuts, plastic clamshell wrappers that various toys and tools were pried out of prior to wrapping, and various balls of ripped paper and packing tape. There's so much trash, I honestly can't believe it. "How can the landfills possibly absorb all this?" I start to perseverate. We're a family that consciously chooses to limit our consumption, but look, there's a mountain of non-recyclable refuse in my home.

I decide that the only sane response to the trash-mountain is to turn it into art, some kind of visual social commentary. I decide that I should chronicle a year (or maybe just a summer, I think, backing away from the idea almost before I've finished having it) of our trash, creating an installation on our one acre by decorating the trees with teabag wrappers, festooning the fence with plastic bags, stacking styrofoam into towering totems. I have the perfect title for the piece: "Family of Five." The journey through our refuse will end with an explosive array of the packaging that arrives unbidden with the boys' birthdays each August.

I then decide with uncharacteristic pragmatism to start the trash-art project once the rainy season is over, and haul several loads out to the garbage and recycling bins, breaking down the cardboard boxes and stashing them in the garage for use as sheet mulch, carefully bagging the peanuts to drive to the UPS store for re-use. Tragically, the UPS store will have already received too many post-holiday peanuts and ask me to come back in a month. My eyes actually start to tear up as I haul the

peanut bag and a cranky Bright Eyes back out to the curb, to
deposit them both back in the car for a dispirited drive home. I
bark at the boys to get in their seats quickly: Mama isn't feeling
very patient. Not throwing things away takes ever so much
more time and effort than simply filling the bin.

In this bleakest of January moments, my imaginary climate
therapist reads my broken expression, tells me that for my own
sanity, I can't do nothing. So on the way home, I drive the extra
two miles to our neighborhood farm to purchase a week's worth
of beyond organic, extremely local, in-season produce (even
though I forgot to pack my canvas bag in the car and will have
to use one of their cardboard boxes to bring it home).

At the farm I do feel hopeful, crouching with Bright Eyes in
her front pack beside the fence of the chicken yard as the boys
joyfully fling sand about in a nearby sailboat sandbox. Bright
Eyes loves the chickens, calls to them with a throaty growl of
happiness as they peck at the carcasses of some half-rotten
pumpkins. But once I've loaded the box of veggies and the
kids back in the car, fossil-fueled despair seeps into my cracks.
I glance in the rearview mirror and catch Bright Eyes in one
of her private smiles: hope. The radio reports more species lost
today: despair. The cornucopia of a tote bag on the passenger
seat reminds me that my kids will be eating kale for supper
(okay, food-processed kale mixed in with their spaghetti sauce,
but a fresh green veggie nevertheless): hope. Hope and despair,
these twin lenses through which I gaze at my children. For me,
these three small people literally embody hope, yet they also
remind me how much can be lost, as they are the ones who
will be trying to forge their lives when those lovely charts Al
Gore showed us will shoot straight up into oblivion. Those
of us already grown will probably scrape by in a recognizable

world for most of our lives, albeit one with a fair amount of turmoil. But my children are the ones who will be living on a new and uncharted planet, one still called earth but with weather patterns and a geographic visage previously unheard of. Oblivious to all this fearsome potential, in fact, to everything but her own happy-chicken song, Bright Eyes clunks off to sleep during the short drive home, drooling head flopped against the side of her seat.

At home, I surreptitiously toss the bag of peanuts toward the back of the garage and hope the boys won't discover it on one of those days when my supervision gets lax, or my attention is otherwise engaged with the baby. Of course, within a week, they do discover it in exactly just such a scenario, which means I do not become aware of their gleeful discovery until the entire filthy floor of the garage is littered with smashed-up bits of Styrofoam, now too soiled and crumbled for the UPS store and destined for the landfill, if I can ever herd them all into the dustpan. I am not particularly nice about this bit of boyhood fun, but I sweep them up myself because I can't stand seeing them there and the boys can't hold back from overzealous broom-wielding, each sweep delighting them further with a cascade of Styrofoam snow. I fill the trash bin with my frustrations, and then anxiously start saving tea bag wrappers for the summer trash show. Individual plasticized tea bag wrappers, freshness-preserving, maybe, but with no use whatsoever beyond my morning cup of non-caffeinated soothing hot liquid. How can we possibly be taking part in a culture that knowingly, intentionally, creates so much garbage? And do I even have any choice in the matter?

Well, there are a million books, articles and websites out there telling me that I do. Telling me how to do it, that I can make a difference, by changing my lightbulbs or my lifestyle, by bicycling and recycling. And I'm doing all that, but I'm also buying too many overly packaged convenience foods and individual tea bags and driving too much in too large of a car. I get so tired of hearing the inspiring story of "look, I did it, you can do it too!" because so many days I feel like I can't. Like I'm doing all I can. Even though I know I should be doing more.

For now, I'm still seeking in vain the hero who can rescue me from my tower of anxiety: that darn climatologist/therapist, who can sit calmly with my neuroses and offer his reassuring prescriptions: if we each just make the changes, it will all be okay. We can do it. All is not lost. Relax, breathe, recycle. Okay, so he's fictional, but that doesn't mean he's not needed, solemnly reflecting back my nervous-mother concerns with gravitas, and reminding me that I am human, I am doing the human-struggle thing (with three small children underfoot, no less), I'm not a Bad Person just because I forgot the canvas shopping bag last week when I was so focused on the darn peanuts. Inhale, exhale, try to remember the bag next time. I'm okay; you're okay; the planet, well, it's not okay, but freaking out doesn't help anything. And if I'm getting too crazy from being trapped in a house with nothing but my own spinning brain and three small people who have no capacity for abstract thought, well, then, it's probably worth the radiation dose to place another call to Brooklyn.

february

Late winter in northern California: rain, some fog, some rain, and oh, a bit more rain. The drainage ditch that runs along the side of my driveway is filling with leaves, sticks, and garbage washed down from where the waste management trucks carelessly spill out bits as they empty the trash and recycling bins along our street. Each morning after I drop the boys at school, I drive in past the growing sludgepile, peering down from my catbird seat in the minivan, wondering who will clean it out, since I'm clearly incapable. This used to be the kind of job I derived great satisfaction from. Now, I can't even imagine how I would navigate the endless downpour, my ten-month old in her frontpack, and the growing pile of cold, wet rotting leaves.

Once I run inside, shielding the baby from the worst of the deluge with my own soggy head, I promptly forget about the drainage ditch cleaning imperative, at least until the next time I drive out. Ensconced with Bright Eyes in our warm, dry cocoon of a house, it's about all I can do to get the laundry from one end of the house to the other, gathering up the various scattered items that need their various, scattered washing methods. I detour into the bathroom to pick up the morning's cast-offs, and am once again reminded what a freak I am.

Here's why 95% of Americans would instantly label me as some kind of fringe radical: I use cloth menstrual pads which I wash and reuse, and have been known in the past to even use the bloody rinsewater to fertilize my houseplants. I don't draw self-portraits with my monthly blood or squat my flow into my garden to experience my one-ness with the cycles of life, but I can't bring myself to create a trashcan full of landfill waste twelve times a year, when soft squares of folded flannel can serve the same purpose indefinitely. Cloth menstrual pads are commercially marketed and sold at my local grocery, so I know I'm not the only one who does this, but the look on my colleague's face at a nursing conference two years ago, when she encountered a small row of drying pads in the bathroom of the hotel room we were sharing, let me know that I was exposing a freakishness about myself.

Most of the people I know would be surprised to hear me describe myself as mainstream. I'm firmly entrenched in what is often referred to as "alternative" culture: organic foods, holistic health care, lefty public radio. My lifestyle is vastly different than that of many of my compatriots; nevertheless, my version of "alternative" has become thoroughly co-opted by the larger culture, and me with it. I drive a fossil-fuel-powered car to the organic grocery store. I have health insurance which covers acupuncture treatments. I use a frequent-flyer credit card to pay for my donations to the local NPR affiliate. "Alternative," like "green," has gone glossy, but really, do I have the strength to fight it? As I step into the mist of the Wholly Bourgeois produce section, I understand that the shiny graphic of my "local" farmer hanging over my head actually represents a dilution of organic farming ideals, but I still buy the groceries, marking myself as a left-leaning but mainstream consumer. I've never been able to fully identify within one of the well-demarcated cultural tributaries that run their own separate course; I can't pass as a full-fledged hippie, nor as a back-to-the-land lesbian, nor even as an eco-academic. So I'm left splashing in the shallows of the mainstream at the same time that I try to resist its current.

In my twenties, I thought I was well on my way toward an off-the-grid strawbale house where I would haul my own water from a well and grow my own food. Then I fell in love with a pragmatic urban artist-type, and everything shifted. If rational judgment weren't clouded by desire, we probably would have just walked away from each other after our first real courtship conversation:

– Could you ever live in the country?
– No. Could you ever live in the city?
– No.

In that moment, in the windy chill of ocean air, I knew that this would be our defining issue for years to come, and even that knowledge didn't send a frisson of fear through me, or a flinch of hesitation. The cold beach gusts just sent us huddling closer together. We laughed, at ourselves and at the future.

It's a blessing and a curse, like so many things, to have a life partner with very different tendencies than my own. I look at my ranch-style suburban house with estranged curiosity and wonder how I ever came to be driving a minivan. Why didn't I choose a partner who would help me set up a biofuel processor in our driveway so I could drive an old Mercedes on fast-food waste? Why didn't I choose a partner who would push me to be a better ecologist, rather than encouraging me to accept comfort and convenience? It's as easy for me to claim the moral high ground of "If it weren't for you…" as it is for grown children to blame our parents for our choices. As easy, and as lame. Maybe no one is helping, but no one is stopping me from setting up my own french fry oil filtering system. It's convenient to be able to externalize all the elements of myself which are happy to turn up the heat rather than wear five sweaters, and call them by The Pragmatist's name. When I am feeling petty and petulant, I am angry with her for not standing on the bank and pulling me out of the rushing water of mainstream culture, but when I am being honest, I have to admit that I was on the bank once, and I saw her swimming, and I chose to dive in.

So I'm in it, driving my kids to sports practice and music lessons just like the typical anxiety-driven mainstream American middle-class mom. I am that mom, actually, even if my menstrual pads are out on the clothesline behind the house. The thing is, I don't submit fully to the force of the current. I don't acquiesce to the entrenched course of accelerating consumption and environmental degradation. I have to believe (to belabor the metaphor) that those of us not drowning can move some pebbles and bit by bit, change the direction of the flow.

It's my mother's way of walking across her farm that has given me this hope. As a younger woman, I often looked at my mother with condescension for her passé version of feminism and her seeming refusal to claim her own power. For years, as she walked from one barn to another, going about the daily chores of farm maintenance, she carried rocks from one area of the creek to a section where the bank was wearing away, one or two at a time in her out-of-style skirt pockets. With a mere half-day of backhoe rental, I knew I could do the task she would seemingly never accomplish. But over time, I have gained an appreciation of her method, and in her honor christened it the Sally Lee School of Incremental Change. What I saw as powerlessness was just patience: she doesn't have to see a result right away, or even soon, knowing that change will come in its own time. Rock by rock, year by year, the creek has slowly shifted back over to its original bed. No need for fossil fuels, nor for the collateral destruction which backhoes invariably create. Just one aging woman, moving a few rocks as she walked by on her way to the barn.

Now that I have three small children of my own, I invoke the Sally Lee School of Incremental Change often. Taking advantage of a break in the rain to go out for a much-needed, baby-entertaining, mother-soothing walk, I look at the composting pile of leaves blocking my drainage ditch, and I push aside the feeling of overwhelm to do just one small bit, push aside one rainboot's load of rotten leaves. Sorting through the hamper of anxieties in my brain, I look at the massive problems of fossil fuels, and though I have yet to make that biofuel car work, I carpool. I consider the massive landfills and my own overstuffed garbage bin, and I take the extra few steps to put the toilet paper tube in the recycling. Maybe not the same month, or even the same year, but change comes.

I always imagined that becoming a mother would push me to action and activism in more public realms—out in the streets, energetically defending what's right in the world to protect it for my children. But for now, at least, my energy goes toward getting diapers changed and food on the table, and it's only late at night when I'm guiltily deleting a mailbox full of calls-to-action! that I remember I'm supposed to be out there making the world a better place. Mothering here in the mainstream, I know I'm too tired to hold up a big protest sign right now—I would just get pushed under the rapids, and I've never been one to hold my breath for very long. But I can be patient, so I'll tread water here near the bank where the current doesn't move too fast, and while I'm at it, I'll put a few pebbles in my pockets.

april

Bright Eyes' roses are blooming, bringing the first year of her life full circle. No, they're not on the rose bush we planted over her homebirthed placenta, California hippie-style, because said placenta is tucked half-forgotten at the back of the freezer still, languishing in typical third-child neglect. We'll plant it someday, when we remember, when we muster up some of those elusive items that such tasks require, namely time and energy.

No, Bright Eyes' roses have come to be called that because they were blooming when I was in labor a year ago. These baseball-sized white popcorn roses are improbably right outside my bedroom window; improbable because our house is built onto a hillside, and so my bedroom looks out into the treetops on the downslope. This particular rosebush, in order to survive, has reached up through the canopy of trees to claim its ration of sunlight. In most locations, a sky-high rosebush would be wasted, its blossoms inaccessible to human enjoyment, and from the ground below one would never suspect the exultant profusion of blooms lurking above the tree limbs. But here is my window, from which I can almost reach out to pick them, and from here, one year ago, I pondered them for many hours as my contractions became less and less manageable.

I was reluctant to leave the bedroom when I was in labor, as it's the room farthest from the neighbors' house, the same neighbors that called the cops, suspecting some domestic disturbance, during my last, nightmarish labor, during which my repetitive, *Psycho*-worthy screams let everyone know that I was definitively not a strong, silent, capable baby-haver. This time, knowing that I lacked the self-discipline to endure the agonies of childbirth quietly, I hid out in the bedroom, encouraging The Pragmatist to distract the boys elsewhere. I paced the short feet of floorspace left between the king-sized family bed, now protected by a plastic sheet tucked beneath our least-cherished bedding, and the padded turquoise birthing tub set up hastily that morning after I woke with surreal surety, announcing, "We're having a baby today, boys." Within this cramped space, I paced, and stopped, and moaned, and stared at the roses.

As skeptical as I've always been of the idea that having a focal point would make the intense pain of contractions more manageable, it worked. Probably because I didn't plan it and wasn't trying to focus on something, I was just, well, staring at the roses. And of course, it only worked until I reached that "I can't do this anymore" stage which was the secret code by which The Pragmatist knew to call the midwife, even though I had expressly forbidden midwife-calling until I was really quite farther along, having gotten very tired of having a midwife around during that first, 49-hour, self-esteem destroying labor.

But by the time the midwife showed up, I had mostly forgotten about those instructions, and about the roses as well, and was just trying to imagine how anyone anywhere is able to endure torture without immediately divulging any and all pertinent information. I knew then that I would never, ever be able to become a spy, because I would have told anything to anyone if it would have made the pain stop. I became unbearably self-pitying and bossy, to which The Pragmatist responded by announcing that if I ever had another baby, she would divorce me unless I got an epidural.

I bellowed and shrieked, and the boys, playing with our friend Rachel in the kitchen, dug out the industrial workman's ear protectors I had bought them to prevent them from incurring early-onset hearing loss from The Percussionist's drum set, and came dancing through the bedroom to show them off. "We're going to Rachel's house to sleep, mom," they giggled in my panting breaks between the contractions, "because we are tired and you... you are TOO LOUD."

"And it would just be too uncomfortable to wear these earphone things to bed," The Percussionist explained.

Before they even completed the five-minute drive to Rachel's house, we'd called them to turn around if they wanted to see the baby come out, as the baby was on the way any second. They got back just in time for Mowgli to state his preference to sleep and immediately do so, and for The Percussionist to see everyone gathered around the birthtub, watching me squatting in such a way as to prevent anyone from seeing or knowing that the head was coming out, except by the fact that I was clutching between my legs and ordering the midwife to "HELP ME BREATHE NOW."

Once the velvet head slid out under my palm, and it was a sliding motion, though that particular verb fails to convey even a slight sense of how incredibly torturous the moment was, I sat back on my haunches and announced, "The head's out," somehow expecting someone to do something about it, you know, like deliver the rest of the baby. But I believe I had cowed them all into such submission that they all froze, waiting for their next order, so I shrugged with intense frustration, and thinking, "for god's sake, MUST I do everything myself?" I pulled my daughter out of me and up into my arms.

So tiny (at 8 lb, 6 oz, the smallest of the three), she nestled there, wet-warm and cheesy, head out of the water, while I suddenly shed the shattering terror of laboring and embraced the more tender terror of motherhood again. With the pain behind me, I could stop fighting, lay down my arms, and surrender to the awe of her first breath of air. Not the most articulate person during times of great stress, I kept breathlessly repeating, "I'm so happy. I'm so happy," over and over, as if I needed convincing of it.

The Pragmatist and our midwife supported me as I stood to move onto the bed for the delivery of the placenta, and I paused, towel-wrapped babe in arms, noticing with intense gratitude the treetop cascade of roses hovering just beyond the window. Even now they remind me that behind pain can lurk unfathomable beauty, just as behind the burning and fear of birthing my daughter, a great healing lay within the experience of bringing her into the world with my own hands. Something that had broken in me during my first too-long, too-scary birth was put back together by that sensation of feeling her muzzle-soft crown swell into my palm, the impossibly smooth skin bloom into her face. For days, weeks after she was born, I repeated the motion, sliding my palm over her soft hair, down her temple, and in doing so I was telling myself without even realizing it at the time: that which is broken can be healed.

It is a message she does well to bring with her, accompanied as she is by my load of eco-anxieties. Her roses are blooming again, and for her first birthday, I've managed to pull a few down from up high to cut for our kitchen table. On her actual birthday, as if aware that I won't be able to remember the milestone without this coincidence, Bright Eyes takes her first reeling steps toward me, my only-yesterday newborn girl, walking. I greet this new child, this toddler, with the same words I used when I first looked into her face one year ago: "Hello, Bright Eyes. I'm so happy." Happy, and scared shitless, but still walking forward, step by careful, brave step.

year two

The world is too much with us; late and soon,
Getting and spending, we lay waste our powers;
Little we see in Nature that is ours;
We have given our hearts away, a sordid boon!

William Wordsworth
"The World is Too Much With Us"

june

Our annual trek to my parents' house in Tennessee reminds me how actually not-hot my California summers are, global warming or no global warming. To combat the crushing humidity of midday, the kids and I quickly establish a post-lunch ritual creek dip. And after the long baking walk across the drought-crisp field, the air of the creek greets us like, well, like a breath of fresh air. A deep inhalation of the water-cooled air on the shady creek bank suddenly makes those ubiquitous (at least in northern California) yoga t-shirts make sense: breathe. Ah, yes. The heat in the field has worked everyone into not just bodily sweat, but into anxious and cranky mindset, which instantly lifts under the cool sated trees. We savor one more gulp of calm, then plunge in, ankle-deep in clear cold ripples, mud clouds billowing up under our heels, minnows and crawdads shooting away from our footfalls.

The boys explore the creek with feckless little-boy abandon, not yet having internalized my stuffed-down maternal fears of snapping turtles and copperheads. They earnestly construct piles of rocks and rotting leaves to dam off channels between platforms of rock, watching with fascination their own power to affect the water's route. Sunlight, bright through summer's lace of leaves, dances madly on the pebbles beneath the surface. A fish appears, slides into shadow. A pencil-thin snake shimmers red-brown against the long grass leaning down into the water. My brain instructs my limbs not to tense, my voice not to rise in fear of this snake who I know not to be poisonous, but who scares me nonetheless. When did I turn into such a wuss? From the safety of my (consciously not-clenched) arms, Bright Eyes laughs and points, as her brothers splash after him, scaring him off in their attempts to get a closer look.

I grew up here, this creek my source of private sanctuary for the difficulties of childhood, a place to hide within deep banks, its calm coolness a balm for the tumults of troubled mind or heart. Now, I bring my children back to this Tennessee valley each year, and each year I unexpectedly receive its healing again. The creek is still here. My mother's piles of rocks keep it contained along its course. It has not run dry, even with the overdevelopment of the surrounding former farmland, even with the stacking of hot dry summer upon hot dry summer. The heron who nested here is gone, his improbably-wide span no longer floating between the close banks, but look, the hawks are still perched on the dead trees in the fencerows. Right here, right now, deer tracks and raccoon prints draw a festive calligraphy along the water's edge. My children know this place the way I know it, from before memory begins. Their as-yet unblemished faces expose a pure joy in connecting their bodies with this water, these rocks.

Of course, the cool relief of the creek does not cure my deep anxieties about the changed world my children will live in, but it does give me a moment to feel that perhaps all is not lost. The small power that they discover today in seeing themselves change the water's flow will grow with them, and I pray that their widening power will be guided by the love of this place, of clean water and animal tracks and cool green shade. I offer a silent prayer to a god I'm not sure I believe in: May the creek still be here for them to watch their own children disappear around the next curve, curious and safe. Please. May they seek sanctuary here, and please, may they be able to breathe.

july

The yearly Tennessee vacation over, we're back at home where I must face the mountain of unsorted mail that The Pragmatist thoughtfully saved for me, set against the picturesque backdrop of my towering collection of tea bag wrappers. I ruthlessly assign most of the mail to the recycling bin, efficiently stack the rest in "immediately" and "someday" piles on my desk, and then come face to face with my day of reckoning. Okay, hello, you said you were going to create this super-activist, fun but shockingly informative trash art installation this summer. Pony up, lady. Summer started three weeks ago, the trip's over, and your first piece is lying limp there at the bottom of the blue bin: "Vacation Mail I." Get off your ass and create already.

Oh, yeah, right. Okay. Right after I have some tea. So in the natural course of my procrastination, I add one more tea bag wrapper to the pile. What the heck is wrong with me (besides the uniquely exhausting jet lag that comes from flying solo with three small children)? Haven't I ever heard of loose tea?

It should be pretty simple, just to switch from tea bags to loose tea. With all my addictive tendencies focused on my tea habit, I would be saving a lot of paper if I weren't unwrapping individually-packaged (for freshness!) tea bags several times a day. And procuring the loose stuff shouldn't even a problem, as I have a friend whose tea house sells an almost infinite variety of teas in bulk. I already bought the stainless steel strainer with the little spring-loaded handle that makes it easy to scoop up the leaves. Yet I still fall prey to the grocery display of boxes of tea bags. They're just so pretty, I want to take them home. And, ugly truth be told, I just want to throw away all these "preserving individual freshness" suspiciously shiny paper teabag wrappers.

Sipping my tea, enjoying the few moments of peace afforded me by the kids' post-vacation rediscovery of all their toys, I admit there's just no way I'm really going to do it, the big, inspired art installation. First, I realize that after I did it, I'd then have a giant pile of garbage to get rid of all at once, which would be a much greater technical challenge than filling the small grey bin each week. Plus, a friend of ours has been living in this little building on our property which I'm quite positive isn't legal as a residence, and who knows who might come to see the art, the whole point being to try and get people to come. So what if one of the people comes and is a county inspector and notices that someone appears to be living in what could best be described as a shed with a composting toilet? What happens to the cool if rustic affordable housing then? Ah, I'd better not.

I'll just keep the pretty, multihued tea bag wrappers until I find some other creative reuse for them. I could string them together into faux Tibetan prayer flags, if I ever get around to it.

In the meantime, I refuse to throw them away. I may not be up to the big art project, but I can at least keep this stack growing on my counter, a visual reminder that for one more day, I've failed to switch to loose tea. Such a little thing, really, but it adds up, and at some point the teabag wrapper population will reach some critical mass on my countertop, a tipping point of guilt where I actually change my behavior instead of just thinking about it.

Then again, if my kitchen counter was free of tea bag wrappers, I might actually feel pressure to use it. You know, for food-related projects beyond preparation of the immediate impending meal. Our garden is starting to come in, reminding me once again that despite our current household obsession with *Little House in the Big Woods*, I'm just not up to Ma's standard when it comes to food preservation. (Not that the long descriptions of food preservation are why this is the first chapter book that has fully engaged Mowgli's attention. I had completely forgotten the equally long descriptions of gun use and care when I checked it out of the library.) It's not clear to me who is more enamored of the *Big Woods* lifestyle, the boys or myself—it seems to seduce each of us with its blend of warm family togetherness, thrilling danger in proximity to the wild, and simple self-sufficiency. "Why don't we live like that?" we ask ourselves and each other as we drift off after bedtime reading.

"Why *don't* we live like that?" I ask myself, scanning the cluttered kitchen and the stack of bills in my hand. Oh, Pa, wouldn't it be more fun to build our own house using only hand tools? Wouldn't it be so much simpler if we all just made our own butter and soap? All these modern conveniences are just so over-rated, I whine as I wait for some toast to pop up in the toaster. Then, as I'm scanning the fridge for the organic no-sugar-added jam, I have to admit that I'm not really cut out for full-on farm life, even if I did manage to can (count 'em) three whole half-pint jars of plum jam last year.

Meanwhile, the kids remain fully engaged with the haul from last Christmas, which tomorrow will again fade from their view and re-blend with the furniture. They are so rarely all three this quiet, I think I'll take the opportunity to organize these bills, and while I'm at it, pour another cup of tea. This old teabag still has some life left in it, and at least I won't have another wrapper weighing on me.

august

With the end of loose summer days comes the beginning of the next chapter: a new school. The Percussionist is moving from the organized but rigid public Waldorf charter school to the chaotic but more progressive public Waldorf charter school for his second year of kindergarten, and Mowgli will join the same kindergarten class for his first year. We had planned for The Percussionist to stay in the original school while Mowgli started at the new one, so we could spend this year deciding which one we would commit to, but faced with the looming prospect of two dropoffs, two pickups, two sets of rules, and two dress codes, it all adds up to too much. So in the final weeks before school starts, we decide to put them both together at the new school, which we find much more open to our needs as a two-mom family.

The unanticipated side benefit of this arrangement is that it frees us up to carpool, as we'll no longer be so tightly scheduled and trying to drop off in two locations at once. Ah ha! I smirk, a real reason to have a bigass car: a carpool-mobile. As a self-righteous carpooler, picking up the (seriously) irrepressible Zach on the way to school, I'm free to take part in the school "green team," the committee dedicated to promoting ecologically sustainable practices such as, you guessed it, carpooling. The green team spends a lot of time debating how we can increase the number of families who carpool. In these conversations, I'm a proponent of shame. It's not so popular of an idea, but I've got a long history with it.

Years ago, my friend Shannon drove up to my house in her brand new-to-her SUV, a red balls-on-wheels Bronco. Jumping down from the driver's seat with a grin on her face, she had a new ass-kicking strut in her walk despite the words coming out of her mouth: "I know, I know, you disapprove, but I need the space for the dogs."

What a stick-in-the-mud I'd turned out to be, that my fun-loving friend couldn't even enjoy her new shiny car in my presence. As if to prove her right, I let my thoughts slip out of my mouth. "I expected better from you," I blurted, to The Pragmatist's shock and embarrassment.

"You can't say things like that," she instructed me later after Shannon had visited awhile and then left us in a cloud of four-wheel drive dust. "It makes people feel bad." And it follows, in unspoken subtext, that 'if people feel bad when they are around you, they won't want to be your friend, and perhaps your raging environmentalism will drive away everyone we like and then we'll be forced to move to some composting-toilet commune just to have any friends. And then we'll have to get a divorce, honey, because I'm a flusher—I like to flush, not shovel, my bodily waste.'

The Pragmatist is a much more socially adept person than am I, so I tend to trust her on these matters. What she's trying to tell me is that Shannon already feels guilty enough for buying something she knows she shouldn't have. In fact, we all feel guilty for doing things we shouldn't. And yet, that doesn't seem to stop us. We feel guilty for driving our cars, for buying too many gifts for our kids, for grabbing a McDonald's meal while on a road trip. We feel guilty, but we still do it, knowing full well that we are contributing to air pollution, global warming, unsustainable levels of consumerism, and toxic agricultural techniques. The guilt clearly isn't working. We point the finger at ourselves, exhibiting our guilt rather than our actions as evidence of our virtues. We can see the hypocrisy in this disparity between our beliefs and our lifestyles, but, as with me and my teabags, the guilt isn't quite enough to push us toward much change. Maybe it's time to give shame a chance.

"Bring back shame," now there's a rallying cry that will draw, um, no one. Despite it's mellifluous sound, the word "shame" dredges up images of those moments we'd rather forget: your shorts suddenly pulled down to your ankles in the middle of the playground by an older kid, the suspicious eyes of a stranger staring down the long aisle of Big Red Bullseye while your children wail on the floor, "child abuser" hissing out from her squint. While I agree that the former scenario holds no draw for me, I can take a longer look at the latter, and get past my initial sense of righteous indignation to discover a world of possibility.

Okay, so the truth is that in that moment, I really hate that woman at the end of the aisle. I mean, *come on*, can't she see that I have three cranky kids and I'm just trying to get out of here? Doesn't she know from the fact that my two older boys are wailing together while I crouch on the linoleum cradling my barely-toddling daughter whose screams are the focal point of this whole scene; can't she tell from this that those pitiful wailing boys rammed the cart into the baby when I set her down and firmly instructed them *more than once* to NOT TOUCH THE CART but then looked away for ten seconds to try and pick up the thing we came here for, for god's sake? And her standing there staring me down is just making me feel shitty and not helping and what is *wrong* with her?

What's wrong with her is that she probably honestly suspects me of having hurt my kids. And what's wrong with me is that she's right. I yelled at them in that scary mom-might-not-love-you-anymore way, and in defense of my youngest cub, I put the death grip on the older ones, the shoulder pinch that brings them to sitting instantly, taught to me by a sweet mild Christian lady whose very, um, "active" son has grown up to be a loving and responsible adult. At the time she told me about it, I was horrified and thought what we all think before we walk out into the world: "I would NEVER do that." And the woman at the end of the aisle is bearing witness to my failure.

Which of course is the real reason I wish she would go away. I am ashamed. I hate feeling like this, so I focus the bad feelings back on her as anger. This is none of her business. But of course I don't really believe it. What I really believe is that if anyone is hurting my children, including myself, it is all of our business to stop the hurting. Everyone's. The government, the teachers, our friends, and even the other Big Red Bullseye shoppers. If she really believes my children may be in danger, she should stay planted there at the end of the aisle glaring until she is reassured that they are safe in my care. And of course it would be better if she walked toward us with a friendly face to see if she could help, or even with a not-so-friendly face to ask the children if they are okay, safe. But she is probably doing the best she can, and in retrospect, I silently thank her. I *should* be subjected to public shame if I hurt my kids. If I am not, there is so little to keep me from doing it again, when the factors in favor of losing it: exhaustion, stress, and the thousandth whine of the day, stack up so high.

The factors influencing us against doing the right thing in so many situations can stack up high. Cost and convenience keep us from buying only organic, local, minimally-packaged foods, our sense of powerlessness to make a difference lets us buy the car we think looks hot rather than the geeky fuel-efficient model. Lethargy and time-stresses, not to mention a recalcitrant toddler, keep me from going back to the car to get my reusable bag when I remember at the checkout that I left it behind the driver's seat. Just this once, I think. Next time, I'll do better, I tell myself as I swing the plastic bag onto the floor of the car.

Driving home, I hear a radio report about how in some city in Ireland, the scourge of single-use plastic bags has been rousted, not by eco-minded legislators, nor even by the nominal fee the stores there now charge for them, but by public opinion. It has simply become socially unacceptable to carry them. "Aha!" I crow. "See, shame works!"

As I drive, I think about SUVs and how often they are referenced in the media and in conversation as bad—bad for other drivers' safety, bad for the environment, just bad, and it seems as though if shame could work in the U.S., there would be no SUV drivers. But then I think about my own minivan, only 19 mpg, and how guilty I felt when we bought it, and how all my friends tried to make me feel better, telling me that I needed it with three kids, that it would keep the kids safe, that I was doing other things for the environment, and I realize that the SUV drivers probably hear the same things from their friends and their inner voices: "You need it for the dogs, for the kids, for driving across that mountaintop in the commercial." Media commentary means so much less than these personal contacts, no wonder the four-wheel drive revolution didn't start to abate until gas hit four dollars a gallon.

I probably won't rally many people to my side, but I'll continue to be a proponent of shame, insofar as I will say a silent and probably belated "thank you" to those who have the courage to face up to my wrongdoing, who continue to expect better from me. For they are the ones who will help me to *be* better. And the next time a friend buys a new car, I'll tell her what I really think if I am disappointed by her choice. I'll tell her, "I know next time you'll choose more carefully." And what I'll be saying is that I am her witness, and I think she can be better than even she herself believes.

And until I muster up the gumption to downgrade both my personal comfort and the physical distance between my too-frequently fist-swinging kids by trading in the minivan for something smaller, I'll stick with the carpool. And I'll try not to feel righteous about our ride-sharing, as my school community witnesses the pack of boys erupting from the van and congratulates our eco-actions. I'll keep looking for that friend, the one who looks deeper and witnesses my shame, the one who will keep asking more of me than I'm asking of myself.

september

Okay, so the attentive reader has probably already figured out that there's more to this "eco-mom wannabe buys a minivan" story. So I'll fess up the whole, humiliating backstory—now that the car is gone, finally. It should be a relief—the hulking grey albatross claimed our driveway for years; now, in one short day, the lurking shadow has been replaced by a large sunny rectangle of open gravel. But I miss it. Tired as I was of the blocked driveway, I miss the way the car made me feel.

In the beginning, that is. I stayed in the relationship way too long, thinking that it would change. But it never did—do they ever? The car just became more like itself, which is to say a useless heap of metal. Still, I miss the feeling. Oh, not the way it made me feel for the last two years: guilty and inadequate, but the way I felt when I first drove it, high with righteousness and pleasure.

Every love story comes with baggage, and mine's easy to guess at: it starts on another single day, just over two years ago. The car was an impulse buy; I blame the hasty purchase on hormones, or panic, or maybe both. Just that morning, the test stick had shown those two dark lines, a new kind of punctuation mark denoting the end of just two children. That day, I was officially pregnant, growing another middle-class American: good for a mother's heart, even good for the Social Security system, but decidedly *bad* for the environment.

Until this moment, we had shoehorned ourselves, our dogs and our two kids into a little Saturn miniwagon, but the fact was, that car could not safely fit the soon-to-be-required three carseats in the back. In the pre-pregnancy days, while I zipped around with my two boys in our little wagon, I often fixated on the other cars on the road. On alternate days, everyone else I saw was driving a 12-mpg monster SUV. The rest of the time, because I live in an extremely eco-conscious community, everyone else was driving a 20-year old Mercedes with a "Runs on veggie oil—no war necessary" bumper sticker. On the SUV days, I buzzed along feeling self-satisfied with our little fuel-efficient wagon, but on Mercedes days, I felt ashamed, entirely dissatisfied, and more than ready to divorce the wagon. I had veggie-oil beater-car lust, and I had it bad.

Our first introduction to veggie cars was our friend and next-door neighbor Molly, who most days could be seen out in her driveway, bent under the hood of her diesel VW Rabbit, her long blond hair dipping into the engine grease as her latex-clad hands adjusted this or that component of her add-on veggie-oil converter. When she wasn't out there, she was usually asking for a ride to her mechanic's. Molly's car broke down all the time, but she had the passion, a fire in her hippie loins that left her undeterred in her pursuit of environmentally benign transportation. When the car was working, she chugged down the lane spewing the tantalizing aroma of McDonald's fries, spicy Indian pakoras, pungent sweet and sour pork, or whatever deep-fryer she had raided that week. Her wafting fragrant afterglow.

I wanted to feel like Molly felt. I wanted the bliss of knowing I had left my lazy and hypocritical petroleum consumption behind me. I wanted to be part of the solution, be the change I want to see in the world, think globally, act locally. I wanted to give my children a planet to live on.

The car purchase turned out to be a textbook shady deal, transacted on a dark suburban street at 10 pm. The guy showing me the car was neither the owner nor the mechanic who had done the veggie oil conversion; he was, however, this totally regular dude who had been using it as a loaner while his own Mercedes got its conversion done by said mechanic. When I tried to register it the signatures didn't match up right and I had to mail the title back to the seller for a signature which still didn't match and the only reason I got the car registered at all is that I'm a middle class white English-speaking woman who was at the DMV with two small children and so provoked great sympathy on the part of the grandmotherly (and also white) clerk who sent it through and said, "Let's just hope the auditors don't catch it."

My mechanic, taking the fatherly role, had warned me from the start to stay away from this kind of thing. How often the older generation just doesn't understand. He even admitted that he didn't get it, why all the same people who had begged him for years to do the cheapest fix on some run-down gas VW were now throwing money at him to revive a faltering diesel Mercedes, all in pursuit of non-petroleum fuel. I should never have introduced them, of course, the paternal mechanic and the love-me, fix-me car. He knew right away that we were wrong for each other. "But you don't understand," I whined. "I can do this, I can make it work."

The thing about the car is that it rescued me from a suffocating sense of guilt about being pregnant again, about bringing another automatically over-consuming American onto the planet. The pregnancy was wretched, The Pragmatist supportive in an ambivalent sort of way, my two sons missing the fun mom they had before morning sickness and preterm contractions took me away from them. But when I drove the car, peering over my growing belly from the sunken front seat, I felt great, strong and earth-motherly, full of life.

My mechanic made the mistake of trying to speak to me rationally. "You need a safe car," he lectured, "what with three kids and all." Safety! Let me tell you something about safety, I silently launched into my repeating internal screed. What good is a bunch of "features," if we are destroying the earth? Am I going to trade the certain overheating of the planet for antilock brakes and the potential protection they provide against potential threats? Can't I achieve the same result with a less "safe" car and a commitment to driving less, therefore limiting both my exposure to harm and my pollution factor? And even if it doesn't have auto-lock seat belts and airbags, isn't it pretty safe to be driving around in a huge heavy chunk of metal when everything else on the road is flimsy fiberglass? "Just fix the brakes," I told him, "and I'll take it from here."

I can exhaust myself, thinking about safety. I read an article years ago describing a hypnosis experiment done with new car buyers. They were asked to draw the car they would like to get and then explain why they wanted it. Most of them drew an SUV-type vehicle and talked about safety, convenience, room for everyone/thing, etcetera. Then they hypnotized them and asked again, and without the inhibitory influence of waking thoughts, they invariably said something like this: "see it's like a tank. The world out there is dangerous with carjackers and who knows what else. In this car I'm safe from the people trying to attack me." Safety, indeed. More like mass psychosis, if you ask me. And the psychosis now has its own logic, with the insurance agent explaining that driving a small fuel-efficient car is really dangerous because all the SUVs will just crush you.

Of course, it's one thing to theorize about different kinds of safety, and it's another to convince your spouse to go along. The decidedly low-risk-tolerant Pragmatist heard the voice of authority pronouncing the car unsafe, and that was it for her. It was in a completely over-the-top response to both her fears and her allowing my dalliance with the Mercedes that I went out and found the used minivan, safety features dripping out its tailpipe, rated "least likely to result in injury" in an accident. I was surmising that I and my veggie-oil chariot could still get away with doing a big part of the family driving when I traded in the wagon for the minivan. It was to be The Pragmatist's security blanket, the family car for when she had the kids or we were all together. And if it was less efficient than the wagon, that was more than made up for by the fact that I would be doing all my driving petroleum-free.

So then what happened? I drove the Mercedes mostly for work, leaving my burnt-salad scent trailing along the wine country roads, pulling my nursing kit out of the spacious if leaky trunk, struggling with windshield wipers that liked to fly off at random moments, but mostly just feeling good about myself. My commitment to the environment was now clearly visible to all who smelled my exhaust or read my "I veg to differ" bumper sticker, my third-child guilt assuaged by the inconvenience of hoisting five-gallon jugs of soybean oil on my widening hip and slowly funneling the oil into my tank.

Of course, after the first few months, things started to go wrong, just as the mechanic had predicted. As the mornings got colder, I would have the disorienting experience of driving a couple of miles, and then suddenly realizing that the gas pedal had become unresponsive. Or, that is, the pedal itself would go down, but nothing happened. I would coast to the side of the road, cut the ignition, hold my head in my hands for a minute praying that I would not have to admit to the mechanic that everything wasn't perfect, and then restart the car. And invariably, the catastrophe of having been driving down the highway in a car with no power would transmute into just a little glitch, as the car would work perfectly for the rest of the day, getting me safely to and from my various house calls. No red flags here, just a little moodiness in the morning.

Until, of course, the days got even colder, and the power problems started closer and closer to the house, and started repeating themselves frequently, with less and less honeymoon period in between. Eventually one day I had to call in to work "carsick" and limp over to the garage, where my mechanic sat looking serenely self-satisfied. "Sounds like you need a new transmission," he gloated, pronouncing this death-toll for the car with nary a flinch. Because of course a new transmission would cost more than the car was worth, and more than I felt we could afford.

"Can't you at least look at it before you decide?" I pleaded.

"Of course, let me have it for a few days."

I was grocery shopping when the dreaded call came in on my cell phone: "Yep, you need a new transmission. It'll be about $3500 dollars. How much did you pay for this car again?"

Damned if I was going to tell him now. "Um, too much, embarrassingly too much."

"Yep, that seems to be what all of you people pay for these cars."

"Anyway, are you sure?"

"Well, Carl wants to tinker with it a bit, he has a couple of ideas. Want me to have him do that?"

"Yes!" I rejoiced at the reprieve, the possibility of salvage.

It was a good thing I had held onto my aging but trusty Civic, the best friend I could always return to with a bruised or broken heart. I whispered my hope that soon I'd be off again in the Mercedes and the loyal Civic just let the words roll right off its dashboard.

A few days later, the shop called again. "Good news."

"You fixed the transmission!" My heart lifted in my chest.

"Not exactly. I spoke with one of these veggie oil people, and he thinks it's just that your oil is too viscous when the weather gets cold."

Of course, I think, and take in a deep joyous breath. Then exhale a bit of frustration and annoyance—I knew I should have found a different mechanic for this car. He's great, my mechanic, for fixing Hondas and other rational cars, but he lacks both the knowledge base and the therapist skills necessary for dealing with veggie oil conversions. Doesn't he understand that these are not mere cars, they are vehicles chosen to carry our hope for us? And doesn't he realize that if the car doesn't work out, despair will begin nipping our heels, and threaten to swallow us whole? Well, whatever, I reasoned, now we know the problem, I can pick up the car and get on with my righteous life, right?

Um, not exactly. "Give me a few days to put it back together, okay?" What could I say: no, give me the disassembled pieces and I'll put it together myself? Unfortunately, I'm one of those women who will at age 55 or 60 finally take a "basic car mechanics" class and start hitting my own forehead over and over, chanting: how could I have gone this long without learning this stuff? But back in high school I was taking advanced French instead of auto shop. Twenty years down the road, I have no idea how the car I drive every day works, and I can't remember more than twenty words of French.

A week later, the call came again. "Looks like you need a transmission after all."

In shock, I stuttered, "But, but we figured it out and that wasn't the problem."

"Well, it won't shift past second gear."

"But it would when I brought it to you!"

"Oh, no, it never shifted reliably. The problem was there, it's just gotten worse."

His confidence somehow silenced me, though inside I ranted: I'm the one who drove this car all over the county for the last eight months. I may not know a transmission from a starter, but I'm not an idiot. I would have noticed if the car wasn't shifting past second gear. Rather than confronting him, I decided not to believe him. I would pick up the car, and he would be wrong. In the warm glow of my tender hands, the car would rev right up the gears and glide me down the highway home.

I picked up the car. Seething but cowed by lingering fear of paternal disapproval, I put the $400 charge onto my credit card. I drove the car home, and of course, it wouldn't go past second gear, no matter how hard I pushed it. I had a defeated irrational sense that there was father-knows-best sabotage in play.

I was still wrestling with the question of what to do next when Bright Eyes decided that the petroleum versus fryer oil debate could wait—she was ready to come out. There's nothing like 14 hours of contractions to push matters of environmental consequence into the seldom-visited clutter-stuffed garage of your mind. Eco-mom was replaced by animal-mom, as I grunted and yowled my cub out in the corner of the bedroom, then stayed in my king-sized nest for a week, nuzzling and mewling to her. The car no longer mattered, as I was clearly never going anywhere again.

But that's the whole thing about having a third baby: there are already two older ones, and they have places to go. Places we can't walk to, since *before* we had kids, we thought it would be nice to have a big enough yard for a pony and garden, since we just didn't figure out *before* we bought a house that we might not want to have to drive to get anywhere. Sure, we could all stay home, but the truth is if I didn't get the two big rowdies off to school and out of my hair for a while I was about start biting and kicking them, quite literally. My teeth were snapping, my claws extended.

Which meant I had to drive, and since my little Civic could no-way-no-how fit three carseats in the back, it meant I had to drive the minivan. Now, I'm way too much of a geek to care whether I look cool or sexy while I drive—I don't have those traditional minivan issues at all. But a mere nineteen war-required, carbon-spewing mpg rating—how could I let myself sink so low? What kind of example was I setting for the kids with that? Clearly, I needed a better solution to the family transportation problem than a minivan and a dead Mercedes. I'm the mom, it's my job to figure these things out.

In search of some resolution for the ailing Mercedes and some balm for my postpartum panic about the state of the planet, I finally screwed up my scraps of courage and confronted my father, I mean, the mechanic. As a mother, I have to model adult behavior to my children. I have to act empowered and brave even when I feel adolescent and timid. So I stalked into the garage with my baby on my hip, stood looking up to the raised platform where he sat in his fort of a desk, and told the mechanic that the car wouldn't go beyond second gear now ("I know") and that before I brought it to him it would go up to fifth without fail ("Not for us, it didn't"). All my pieced together courage just bashed into the brick wall of his sureness and shattered to pieces. I slunk home with my tail between my legs and quietly found another mechanic with a better bedside manner, who repeated the terminal diagnosis. At this point, the car was not going to last without a new transmission, and even then no guarantees.

I couldn't really let go, hoping somehow, something would change. Even with the car limping along, my self-esteem rose each time I got behind the wheel. This was who I wanted to be. In order to get through the days of watching my children grow, I needed hope. I needed to believe that we can make the changes needed to stop killing the planet. I needed the car. It sat, and sat, and got covered with leaves, and then I cleaned it, and then it sat and sat and got covered with leaves and dust, and then I cleaned it and took pictures of it to try and sell it. It sat collecting gravel dust and growing mold all over the dash, and I put up optimistic flyers: Mercedes for sale, drives on veggie oil, needs new transmission, best offer. I wanted to write

"Free to good home" but who knows who might have taken it, just because it was free. Maybe they wouldn't have taken care of it and loved it if they didn't have anything invested.

I certainly had a lot invested, and even I wasn't taking care of it, neglecting it more and more as the demands of three kids drained my energy. So the car sat and sat, collecting spiders and rodents, and then in a burst of spring sunshine I bought it a new battery and took it to the carwash. I defiantly drove it to another town on the absurd premise that maybe it needed exercise. I drove back in 3-minute chunks, the engine smoking because some of the engine's former rodent residents had chewed through a tube leading from the radiator. I saw how I'd grown in the relationship when I looked at the tube and thought, "I can fix that myself!" After all, I'd installed the new battery solo after exhausting my allotment of AAA calls in my various scattered attempts to revive my righteous ride.

As time passed, the theoretical thrill of saving the planet reshaped itself into a practical guilt at having failed. There I was with three kids and a minivan, pretending to myself that I was somehow different. My friends whose restaurant had been a reliable source of recycled fuel went out of business. The radio reported that evermore rainforest was being cut down to grow soybeans for biofuels. Diversion of land from food crops to fuel production was reported to be contributing to famine. Where's the righteous in that? I knew the car wasn't good for me anymore. I admitted to myself that I needed to move on.

But what do you *do* with it, when you know it's over? Post it on Craig's List and warn away everyone who shows interest, recognizing in them the optimism you have lost? Consider: what is the most environmentally friendly use for a dead car? Answer your own question: recycling, probably—find someone who wants it for parts. Irrationally procrastinate dealing with figuring out how to do this. Keep secretly hoping for a miracle, that wishing will conquer all, and you will magically reinstall the bank of carseats across the Mercedes' back seat, abandoning the minivan to its petroleum fumes.

No miracles occurred, but a letter flew in on the wings of fate, or so it felt. It was convenient, this "yes, this is the right answer" feeling. A convenient solution to a spectacularly inconvenient situation. The letter told me that our local air quality board was trying to get older diesel cars off the road, and they would pay $600 for the car if I could drive it as far as the "auto recyclers." Hurrah, I sighed, my problems were solved—I could unblock the driveway *and* reduce pollution. I was then distressingly informed by friends that the "recycling" is not very ecological: the car would be crushed without removing usable parts and then shipped to China(!) where it would be used for some kind of construction application. This information stalled me for a while, as I grieved again the feeling of rightness that had originally come with the car and then reappeared with the letter. Even in this final process, I could not end up feeling good about my choices. I sold the veggie oil conversion system off the car and hobbled the Mercedes to the designated shop where they took it off my hands. As in any other overdue breakup, I felt both relieved and culpable.

The car is gone. I'm guilty of having failed to rescue my conscience from the ecological consequences of reproduction. My penance is to drive around in a gas-guzzling minivan, each day my anxiety mounting about the unsustainability of my suburban lifestyle. How will I explain to the children that it's just too easy to put off getting a more efficient car when what you're driving is so damnably comfortable, with automatic everything and enough room to separate people likely to hit each other? How can I justify this continued exploitation of the earth's resources? I fret, I worry, I try to drive less, and then we pile in the car to go to school, to music class, to Little League. It's now my heart that seems to need a new transmission, as I limp along as if without power, day after day letting myself be the thing in the world that needs changing.

I can only hope that in a few months, my heart will start to mend, and like a middle-aged divorcee, I'll start thinking, just thinking, of dabbling in the pool again. For now, I'm not ready to jump into anything, but I do go online and check out the personals: 1986 Merc 300SD VO seeking MWF for mutual affection and enlightenment, 2004 Prius looking for sporty female companionship, new NEV seeks long-term commitment. I scan Craig's List just to browse, but getting closer and closer to trying again, this time with the clear eyes of one who has survived heartbreak but not entirely given up hope. In the meantime, the minivan dominates the gravel patch, singing its sugardaddy siren song: life can be this easy.

early october

As we all settle into the school year, a syncopated rhythm of school-sitter-work-play presses us forward from week to week. I sign up for night and weekend shifts at work so I can be home with the kids as much as possible, collecting the scattered brown-soled socks, loading up the crock pot in the mornings, harvesting the last of the still-green tomatoes to fry up. After the kids are asleep at night, I read the latest books about how and what and why we should all be eating to make the world and our kids healthier.

Inspired, I try to wean myself from my beloved Discount Organics Chain Store, stocked as they are with highly processed, centrally-distributed, industrially-produced organic foods. I boil our chicken bones and onion skins into rich stocks and freeze yogurt cartons of soups to have on hand for those hectic nights when I would normally serve frozen pizza for supper. I soak beans, freeze bags of the last-of-season berries collected with Bright Eyes while the boys are at school, her greedy hands claiming five blackberries for each one that makes it into my repurposed yogurt carton "pail." I sign up on the waiting list to buy a quarter of a cow, a half of a pig, locally and biodynamically raised. I read labels, I bring my reused plastic bags to the grocery store to fill from the bulk bins. All of this makes me feel good about myself, but it also makes me very, very tired. I'm trying to "do it right," but it's just not always clear what's right, except that it almost invariably boils down to this: more work for me.

I'm spending many hours trying to maintain a set of priorities that are clearly important if you think rationally about how we should not only be eating, but also treating the planet. I seek out local, organic, biodynamic, but the more I read, the more complex the issues become. I can almost remember a time when a chicken was a chicken, and an egg was an egg, and the answer to which came first simply depended on whether you believed in evolution. Ah, the good old days. Nowadays, the chicken-and-egg business is awash in adjectives and hyphens; something as basic as an egg carton teems with descriptions pointing the unwitting consumer in all sorts of labyrinthine directions. When did everything get so complicated?

I suspect that at some point in the not-too-distant past, the word "natural" actually had a meaning shared by most of the population. In the new millennium, "natural" is a throwaway— you have to add "all-" to wring any value at all from it, and it's still pretty parched. As our choices have expanded, and sustainability in agriculture has begun to enter the popular consciousness, we are barraged by the marketing of "natural" foods, nowhere more apparent than in the egg aisle. But as more and more people want foods produced by humane and earth-friendly methods, the supply doesn't seem to meet the demand. Those truly all-natural hens can't lay fast enough. Enter the funhouse of the modifier.

There was always large, extra-large, and jumbo, the egg-producers having beat Starbucks in the race to label everything as superlative by several generations. And white or brown. That used to be the extent of it, two simple decisions, size and aesthetic preference. Now there are moral decisions to be hashed out as you choose between free-range, cage-free, Omega-3, family-farmed, no-gmo, veggie-fed, hormone-free, organic, locally-owned, antibiotic-free, artisan-made, sweatshop-free…(oops, I think I got out of the egg cooler just there at the end). What with the large and fine print cluttering the egg cartons, it's no wonder there's usually a bottleneck right at the egg section of my local grocer, as my fellow bewildered customers try to figure out if Susie's Family Farm or Paradise Organics is the right choice. Does Susie treat her workers well, we wonder? Has Paradise been bought out by some evil corporation? Are ANY chickens ever given hormones, or are the egg folks just borrowing a bit of anxiety-calming rhetoric from the red-meat folks? And does any of it really make a difference to the chickens?

From an aesthetic and ethical standpoint, I want to buy eggs and meat from chickens that were raised the way I picture chickens in my mind, strolling about the farmyard magically unmolested by attentive herding dogs. These chickens populate Bright Eyes' cardboard books in plenty, pecking at the green tufts of grass with their chicks trailing behind. These chickens look happy, expressing their inner "chicken-ness" by partaking of the activities dictated by their natures: scratching, catching bugs, and whatever else a self-realized chicken does. In a real world, these enlightened chickens would even lay eggs with naturally high amounts of Omega-3 fatty acids and would be resistant to disease because they are healthy and unconfined, living out the picture that "free-range" produces in my mind.

I do manage to find some of these storybook chickens at the farmer's market set up in the parking lot of our town plaza, slowly winding down as the late fall replaces heirloom tomatoes with delicata squash in the stands. The fairytale farmer is youthfully handsome and idealistic, flaunting a notebook filled with photos of the hens wandering his acreage, basking in the sunshine and freedom of sustainable farming methods. I gush with excitement: finally, food I can feel unreservedly good about feeding my children! I happily hand over an exorbitant $5 for a dozen guilt-free eggs and start to walk away, but am lured back by the perfect poultry in the pictures. "Do you happen to have any broilers?" I venture. "Just one left," he grins. He hoists the sole remaining chicken out of his freezer and looks at the label on it: "Four pounds, okay with you?" I return his wide-open smile as I hand him a twenty, taking the chicken and dropping it into an old plastic bag as I joke, "Can't you find a bigger one in there?" pointing to the now-empty freezer. There is an awkward pause after he pockets the bill I just gave him and says, "Thanks. Hope to see you again." I am still smiling politely, waiting for the change he does not seem to be getting for me. In my unsureness about how to handle the situation, my eyes scan the booth, and only then do I actually read the little chalkboard which gives the prices of his various vegetables, listing at the end: chicken, $5/lb. Four pounds at five bucks a pound, shit, that's TWENTY DOLLARS! I just bought a twenty dollar chicken, and I'm way too embarrassed to hand it back after I have been falling all over myself telling him about how great it is how he's doing all the right things, how I wish more people were doing it like him. I grin one last time to cover my confusion and regret, and turn away, swinging the bag with the $20 chicken from one hand.

Now bereft of cash, I wander away from the produce stalls over toward the lawn where several families are picnicking, enjoying the warm weather's last gasps. My own kids are clamoring around in the general mélange of children, and I stop by to check on them and say hi to the other parents I know. At each blanket I hold up the paltry-seeming bag and flatly announce, "I just bought a $20 chicken," my shock temporarily trumping the embarrassment I will start to feel shortly.

The sheer indulgence of having spent twenty dollars on one chicken weighs on my stereotypically middle-class scale of guilt, but it's balanced by the fact that I realize it probably represents the true amount of money a chicken is worth in the world that I, with my liberal ideals, would wish into existence if I had the requisite power to do so. In a world where all workers are paid fair wages to ensure a decent standard of living, in a world where the chickens are outside of their efficient "cage-free" warehouses actually eating wild insects and acres of grass instead of processed chicken feed with its list of suspect ingredients, in a world where the farmer values sustaining the earth over profits, a chicken would cost at least $20. My $20 chicken would probably be in the bargain basement of such a world.

And I have to admit, to my untrained palate, fed for years on plump "free-range" roasters that probably never saw sunlight, my $20 chicken tastes pretty bargain basement: rangy and a little tough. Probably, just as with grass-fed beef, truly free-range chicken requires we adjust our cooking methods as well as our taste buds. I'd be happy to make the adjustments, I'm just not sure I can afford it. The "right" solution here would probably be to do some math: figure out how much I spend on chicken and use the same amount to buy only this truly sustainable version. Which would mean less chicken, but less guilt. Or raise my own free-ranging fowl in my back yard, an option I consider only until I mention it to the city-bred Pragmatist, who lays down a clear line in the chicken scratch: if we have chickens, we can eat their eggs but not them. No neck-wringing *chez nous*. I make a half-hearted attempt to woo The Pragmatist into the possibility of setting up our own slaughter house. "*Coq au vin*," I murmur seductively. "*Poulet provencal.*" No go. She used to swoon when I spoke French to her, but somehow my murderous plot isn't having the same effect as romantic renderings of lines from *Jules et Jim*.

I love that she gives me this out. Although chicken is my kids' favorite meal, and I do want us to eat in the most sustainable way possible, I was already developing a sense of dread about the moment of killing itself. Wring or chop? Of course, my pint-sized barbarians would probably love the literal sight of the proverbial headless chicken. In one of my most vivid memories of my semi-agrarian childhood, the seeming impossibility of that flapping, running bird-sans-head provoked my older brother to a hurricane of laughter. I recall inching backwards, fascinated but afraid, even though the bird's main weapon was lying still attached to the tiny head near our chopping block. So I'm not in denial that the meat we eat comes from creatures that once lived and breathed, it's just that I'd rather outsource the slaughter function. Back to the butcher counter for me, at least until the farmer's market reopens in the spring, when I'll have to grapple with my conscience and my wallet both.

In the meantime, we're eating a lot of eggs, without reading a lot of fine print. I've recently discovered that I can buy eggs from a neighbor, cheaper than the market eggs, packaged in battered recycled cartons festooned with adjectives no longer tied to the particular eggs within. These eggs, with their irregular sizes, muted palette of blues, greens and tans, and bits of straw still stuck underneath, feel somehow more real than the grocery store version—those homogeneous soldiers lined up ready to march through USDA inspections. With the homegrown version, I don't need a barrage of modifiers to soothe my maternal health concerns, my environmental anxiety, and my animal welfare fears—the chicken herself was underfoot as I climbed up the neighbor's porch steps to see how many extras they had today, and she looked plenty happy and healthy to me.

I guess the only thing that could be better would be that family-run, collaboratively-built, no-slaughter, egg-only, recycled-materials, beyond-organic, fully guilt-free henhouse I haven't given up planning. I've got some old boards behind the garage. But until I find the time for a construction project, it'll be me and the kids walking down the road to the neighbor's, bringing our empty egg cartons for a refill. The angled sun reflects off their hair as they crouch giggling among the roadside weeds, lying in wait to burst out and evoke a well-practiced screech from me. And as we make our way past fennel and shriveling blackberry, dried-out Queen Anne's lace and drooping wild mustard flowers, for at least until we get back home, life seems simple again.

late october

It's a good thing that I love *The Runaway Bunny*, Margaret Wise Brown's classic picture book about the bunny child trying to hide from his mother by transforming into various different forms, each of which that clever mother rabbit discovers through her own metamorphosis. If I didn't love it, I'd be insane by now with the endless repetition, the gracefully chubby finger pointing tirelessly at each page, the insistent "ma, ma, MAAA, MAAA" when my mind yet again wanders away from "Yes, there's the baby bunny. Yes, there's the mama bunny." Sometimes my mind has drifted toward the kitchen: what's for dinner? When will those dishes hop out of the dishwasher? But as often I have floated into the watery paintings, the timeless ink drawings of that little bunny replete with a premature desire for independence, his hiding places in plain sight to lure his mother's protective force to him.

I remember loving this book as a child, and now that I have seen the ages at which my own children fall into these pages with abandon, I realize that these must be among my earliest memories. I remember being so proud when I found the baby bunny in the crocus, thrilled by the danger and freedom in his pastel wings. Now Bright Eyes, not yet two, pulls it out of the boardbook basket several times a day, pushing it into my lap as soon as I consent to stop sorting laundry and join her on the rumpled couch.

My sister-in-law doesn't read this book to her kids; she finds it creepy. "Stalker-mom," her two-word description. I tried to laugh at that, but it came out so obviously forced that I had to admit to disagreement. "I, um, think that's maybe a more adult interpretation?" I stutter, trained by my southern upbringing to avoid conflict at all costs. "I kind of think maybe it makes kids feel safe, er, protected?" We drop the subject, the final word her opinion that "I will come after you" is a freaky thing for a mother to say.

I have recently been saved from nagging doubts about my imposition of stalker-bunny on my kids by Margaret Edson's thoughtful play "Wit," in which a dying academic is read to by her intellectual mentor in her waning moments. The improbable choice for this final text the simple words of Margaret Wise Brown, "Once, there was a little bunny who wanted to run away…" Of course, without stellar performers this theatrical moment could be revolting treacle. But in the right voice, "if you become a bird, I will be the tree that you come home to" can turn out to be magically transcendent. The mentor muses as she sees the cancer-ridden patient has fallen asleep to her words, "ah, an allegory for the soul." Aha! I shouted triumphantly to myself. See, it's not stalker-mom, it's *God*. And I realize how deeply my sister-in-law's devout atheism separates her worldview from my own.

Not that I believe in God, at least any particular god with a capitalized name. I mean, I may believe in an idea *like* God, but if I don't subscribe to any religious mythology, can I really be said to believe? One of the things I love and hate about the writer Anne Lamott is the belief in grace that warms her writing, a silvery threading through the edges of her essays that gathers them up into bow-wrapped gifts. I love it because reading her work empowers me to get out of bed the next morning, and I hate it because the strength of her grace rests in her faith. My clear yen for grace belies my own lack of faith; nevertheless, the faith continues to elude my conscious self.

As a non-believer, or at least a nonspecific believer, I never know where to sit. I was baptized and confirmed as a protestant Christian, I dabbled in Buddhism as a young traveler, I took the college courses surveying the world's religions. As a lesbian feminist, I never found a home with any of the solitary male godheads, but goddess-worship felt forced, like a veneer overlay. I dipped into Wicca, feeling a true connection with my spiritual self most strongly in relationship with nature, but the motley moonlit circles and costuming felt ridiculous. I took my kids to a liberal new age spiritual center briefly, but the theology seemed too self-serving and, well, wealthy. Nevertheless, when the discussion turns to People of Faith, I always feel like those should be my people. For if they aren't, what does that make me? A person of faithlessness? Straight up atheism is way too hardcore for me—I don't want to read the world as full of stalker moms. And I can't shake the sense that there is a mysterious intelligence higher than mine, and it isn't Noam Chomsky.

I think we need to christen a new category: People of Doubt. Those of us who can't articulate a personal theology but don't rule out the possibility of an inarticulate one lurking beneath the surface. We would be the swing-voters, the sought-after independents if religion and secularism devolved into political rivalry (more than they already have). Not entirely agnostic, the People of Doubt can be wooed. We have a sense of mystery and desire for engagement, and we like the idea that if we become a sailboat, something will blow us in the right direction. We want to believe there is someone watching over us, tracking the safety of our souls, but we don't have a name for it, so we don't feel sure. We cling irrationally to our unhinged hope for grace. We read *The Runaway Bunny* to our children, over and over like a mantra.

And from within our doubt, we seek a sense of knowing what is right, what is wrong. We feel it: for me, the seeming wanton destruction that we humans are wrecking on the earth feels not just ethically but spiritually wrong. A bad thing greater than regular, forgivable human frailty. But who do I suppose has the power to offer and withhold forgiveness? Me? Please, no. Without a definite theology, how do I discern the difference between venial and cardinal sin? Am I supposed to figure this all out *on my own*? Yikes. I'm left relying on an intuitive sense of justice, of virtue, of morality, hoping against hope that something larger than me might be guiding my inner compass. Hoping that someday that larger something, that grace, will track me down, here in my mortal hiding place.

My two sons affectionately recall their own *Runaway Bunny* days as they are re-immersed thanks to my toddler daughter's obsession. "Have a carrot!" they squeal each time I offer one from the vegetable drawer, and their big-boy kindergarten laughter already hints of a time when they will no longer stay here and be my little bunnies. When that happens, I only hope that they will hide in plain sight on the rocky mountainside of adulthood, so that even if their mother can't climb to them, they will be open to grace finding them, from somewhere.

november

I stare down the drab linoleum hallway with the vacancy of late afternoon exhaustion as I'm waiting for Mowgli's *tae kwon do* class to end. He appears out of nowhere in his belted black uniform, holding his finger up into the wind to see which way Mom's mind is blowing. Cookie or no cookie? The martial arts studio shares a building with a cookie store, enticing the worn-out kids in for a post-workout pick me up. My son's thoughts are as readable as if he had tickertape running along his forehead: cookie cookie cookie, I hope she'll say yes, cookie, cookie, what kind should I get? cookie cookie cookie smells so cookie cookie? After all, he is only five, despite his high stretched kicks and clean blocks. My distracted brain pulls into focus: oh, shit, now what do I do?

When The Pragmatist and I first moved to this town, a year before The Percussionist was born, the cookie store perched right on Main Street seemed like a confirmation that we had made the right choice—this was a town where kids would be happy, embraced not only by a cookie walk-by window

on Main Street but by child-friendly businesses, witnessed by
the plethora of "Thanks to our sponsors" sports team plaques
outgrowing their wall space in the cookie store, mechanic's
shop, and the mom and pop grocery. The cookie store's cookies
themselves were delicious, soft with a crunchy border and
available in a panorama of varieties: the standard chocolate chip,
oatmeal raisin, peanut butter, and ginger snap array spiced up
with a pale amaretto crisp, a deep espresso mocha chip, and
even a homely "backpacker" goulash of a cookie with a list of
healthy ingredients so long it made you forget that the first
one was sugar.

We happily treated ourselves to the cookies for years, a
perfect lift during a long afternoon of errands, not only guilt-
free (hey, we were pregnant, we were breastfeeding, we needed
the calories) but feeling as if we were contributing to our
local economy and community. And then one day, perhaps in
reaction to a nasty rumor, or perhaps just to torture myself, I
asked to look at their ingredient lists, which they keep handily
in a binder just behind the counter. And if it was a nasty rumor,
then it was true, because I learned that our favorite treats,
our bribes for good behavior to get through those midday
meltdowns, were all made with margarine.

Okay, okay, so I'm perfectly healthy at 39 and I ate plenty
of margarine as a kid, gobs and gobs of it, sneaking slices of the
stuff plain when my mother turned her head. But now we avoid
it like a plague, or more accurately, like a plaque in the coronary
artery. The boys' first babysitter, Molly of the deep-fried VW,
taught them to understand that "hydrogenated fats" was a
term equivalent to "no." Sure, we let their aunt sneak them
Oreos from time to time (like every time they see her), but the
cookie store is *our* choice, something we have introduced, and

the refined sugar and non-organic white flour are bad enough, right? Now that we have to add probably genetically-modified, hydrogenated vegetable oils to the equation, does the result change? Is the cookie store now on the "avoid altogether" list, about ten steps down from the "only if you've been really good" list?

I start using the *tae kwon do* hour to walk a block over to the teahouse if I am in a cookie mood, or, more rarely, if the kids have actually earned a treat. The teahouse makes their cookies with real live local butter, saturated fats for sure, but none of the demonic trans-fats that have been banned from all god-fearing homes. Of course they don't have the selection or the fantastic mixture of chewy and crisp that the cookie store flaunts in their window, but I can feel good about my choice, even better since the one-block trip sometimes feels like an incredible journey of epic proportions with an obstinate toddler and an over-tired six-year-old non-martial artist in tow. Bright Eyes has perfected Gandhian non-violent resistance, flaunting her budding activist skills by willfully collapsing in the not one but two crosswalks between the *tae kwon do* studio and the nonhydrogenated cookies, while The Percussionist tends to obliviously wander so close to the edge of the sidewalk as to cause concerned motorists to swerve out of the path of his seemingly likely fall.

With my health-food cookies in hand, I am the Righteous Mom, surrendering ease and convenience for the health of my children and the good of the planet—you can almost see me raising my arms for a triumphant bicep flex. Righteous Mom rocks, singing sanitized Ani DiFranco tunes to the wee ones, building her own off-the-grid cobb house as she celebrates her garden's ample harvest by canning enough homegrown fruits and vegetables to last through till next spring. Okay, so maybe not, but at least she drags the reluctant two siblings of Mowgli a few hundred feet for healthier cookies. And then Righteous Mom can rest for a few minutes, secure in her sense that she has Done the Right Thing.

Until, of course, Righteous Mom comes face to face with the other moms waiting for *tae kwon do* pick-up, the "Good-enough" moms, and realizes that not only do they appear more relaxed than she does, but their children seem exceptionally mellow, at ease, happy. Righteous Mom's kids are still whining from being dragged across the street too many times. The Good-enough Moms' kids are clutching crescents of crispy cookie, chocolate chip smears scrawled on the corners of their mouths. They have not noticed that their Good-enough Moms didn't make a Herculean effort to protect them from hydrogenated fats, they just wondered about, and felt a little sorry for, my kids as they were hauled away from the close and convenient cookie source.

Today my friend Selena, spokeswoman for the Good-enough Moms, is celebrating having found a daycare which will accept both of her children while she works. It's not the organic, vegetarian, only-wooden-toys, bucolic preschool where we both sent our kids last year, but an in-home daycare closer to her house, with longer hours. "It's not perfect," she admits without reservation, "but it's affordable and convenient and good enough." She does not cringe with shame when she says this, her shoulders are square and she shrugs them, adding, "and sometimes good enough is just that: good enough." Hearing this, with two tired kids collapsed on the hall floor at her ankles, Righteous Mom starts to wonder when "righteous" ends and "uptight" begins.

In search of balance, I let the pendulum swing the other direction. I backpedal on the no-cookie-store directive, allowing the margarine cookies when no other option seems possible without undue stress. Once the rule has been relaxed, the definition of "undue stress" gets looser and looser until it morphs into the equivalent of "inconvenient in any way whatsoever." Righteous (read: Uptight) Mom figures out how to join the tribe of Good-enough (read: Cool) Moms and kick back at the nearby library during class time, grabbing a handful of cookie store cookies when class lets out (if cookies are warranted, which is not all the time, despite my raging sweet tooth and the pleas of the pack). And it turns out that everyone in the family can be more relaxed when I'm not *trying* so frigging hard, taking each little decision so seriously, as if my children's future health and happiness depended on this or that particular detail. I start to wonder if sometimes the right thing to do may be to not work so hard at Doing the Right Thing.

Until, of course, the day when the pendulum inevitably begins its swing back. With a mixture of guilt and relief, I have yet again succumbed to cookie store temptations, and am lurking in the hallway for the last few minutes of class clutching my distinctive black and white cookie-sized bag, when one of the other *tae kwon do* moms strolls up. As the class ends, pleas for please-just-today-chocolate-chip-please wisp through the still closed door. The other mom turns to me and rolls her eyes at how tired we all are of the unvarying after-class cookie discussion. "I *always* say no and he knows it, but he asks anyway," she gripes, as I slide the hand holding my cookie bag further behind my hip. Having noticed neither my cookie bag nor my burgeoning guilty conscience, she continues, "And I wouldn't let him have those cookies even if it wasn't just before dinnertime. I mean, it may just be a nasty rumor, but I heard they use *margarine!*"

december

Christmas is coming. Santa fever started way back in October, when The Percussionist requested a Santa Claus costume for Halloween, "because I love Santa so much." Several yards of red fleece (perfect for the not-quite-adequate seamstress because it is, as they say at the fabric store, "very forgiving") and fake fur transformed him into the toast of neighborhood trick-or-treating, eclipsing Mowgli's piratical growls and even Bright Eyes' undeniable cuteness in her bunny suit. "Oh, look! It's Santa!" passers-by and candy-handers would laugh, this displaced character surprising with his two-months-early appearance, "Santa came for Halloween this year!" The Percussionist's obvious pleasure in being the temporary star of the sidewalk almost made up for the fact that I was complicit in the purchase of what, in the end, was actually a fuzzy sheet of red plastic disguised as "fabric." I'm against plastic. And now the other Santa is heading our way, and the onslaught of plastic will begin for real.

Here's the thing: plastic is bad. Really bad. Oh, we all knew it must be pretty bad when they started coming out with those commercials in which a careening toddler knocks into the legs of a table, causing a domino effect scenario in which a full 2-liter soda bottle flies off the table onto the floor in close proximity to said toddler and the bottle harmlessly bounces, making us all blink with the horror of what might have happened if it had been a glass bottle shattering, throwing off shards into innocent little feet, legs, eyes. If the plastic industry is buying prime time ad spots to tell us how great plastic is, we can be fairly sure that the stuff is bad.

Unable to squelch my habit of fixating on Doing the Right Thing, I read too much, about manufacturing byproducts, about recycling processes, about waste streams, all that discouraging stuff, so I'm way past fairly sure. And "bad" probably doesn't really encapsulate it. "Evil incarnate" comes to mind, except you can't really use the word "incarnate" to describe something so intensely lifeless.

I'm not saying that plastics don't have their good points. I'd be up a creek without my Tupperware. And my raincoat. And the super-cute nylon dress I wore to my friend's wedding, not to mention the control-top pantyhose that made it fit right. Oh, and the pipe that runs from our house to the septic tank. And, um, a good portion of my car, without which I would be stranded on an acre I'm not yet capable of using to produce enough food for a family of five. Oh, and the Santa suit. So I probably shouldn't be bad-mouthing plastics, lest the more recent fillings in my teeth leap out in rebellion, or my computer keyboard turn against me.

Okay, so there's a part of me that believes we should just find a way to get rid of ALL the plastic, but I'm aware that it's the same part of me that over-romanticizes the *Little House on the Prairie* books. So if I can't advocate for getting rid of ALL the plastic, how about just the unnecessary stuff? Like, um, the toys. Always going for that "super-mom" title, I pick as my personal no-plastic mission the main source of my children's pleasure, their toys. Oh, and to add insult to injury, I tack on plastic yogurt containers. Since of course, individual-sized flavored yogurts are one of the grown-up world's great gifts to childkind.

And now, Christmas is coming, and in our house, in our particular secular subset of middle-class American culture, Christmas means gifts. Now, I put a lot of thought into gift-giving, and I believe that the best gifts are those in which the giver's and receiver's values intersect. Not all gifts are the best ones. With a gift, there is always the opportunity for the foisting of your values on someone else. Or, sometimes, there can be the acquiescing to someone else's values, which can be supremely romantic if it makes your wife happy, but ultimately feels a bit morally cheap. But the main thing is, it's nice to give gifts that the receiver actually wants. And most of what my kids want is plastic.

When the boys were around the age Bright Eyes is now, I drafted (encouraged by a lefty mothering magazine and with resigned agreement from The Pragmatist) a letter about gifts, addressed to my generous but not always eco-minded "dear friends and family." I never sent it, of course, the polite southerner in my core trumping the earth mother protecting her territory from unnecessary consumer goods. But now, inspired by Bright Eyes' growing stack of redundant and totally unneeded toys, I haul it out of my laptop's archives and try again. It reads as follows:

"I am besieged by competing values, and have therefore delayed sending this letter for literally years. Parenting has brought me up against daily choices about which values I will prioritize in any given moment. Do I espouse pacifism or encourage individual expression when it involves swordplay? Do I insist on healthy organic meats for my developing children, or do we show good manners by eating whatever is offered? Do I gratefully accept gifts, or do I try to maintain a home environment which reflects our values? It's this last one which has prompted this letter. I have read several articles about this dilemma, a strange side-effect of our consumerist, middle-class economy: too many toys. Toys overwhelming the rhythm and tone of the home.

"Here is what happens: I read. I read about plastic manufacturing, about waste streams, about outsourcing pollution, and all this reading makes me a little manic about how we can leave a smaller, less toxic footprint. Having *three(!)* children requires that we examine our use of resources even more closely, that we try even harder to teach them their responsibilities to the planet and all the people living on it. And so we look at our home, at the objects we surround ourselves with, and ask what they are teaching our children about making sustainable and ethical choices in this era of constantly accelerating change and frightening predictions.

"Okay, so get to the point, already. All this explanation serves as a preface to our request that you, our friends and family, the people who love our children and whom our children love, try to think beyond the excitement of opening a large box, think beyond the fun of having lots of stuff, and choose gifts which will blend in with the home environment we are trying to create, one which encourages thoughtful, careful consumer choices, and teaches that objects are not the source of happiness.

"What does this mean? For one thing, cut down or eliminate plastics and synthetic materials. Our children know that we do not buy plastics if other choices exist, to reduce pollution and waste. Also, plastic toys are usually difficult or impossible to fix when they break, contributing to our cultural myth of disposability. It's confusing for our children to receive gifts from people whom they love and respect, when those gifts represent something we've told them is harmful to the planet.

"On the other hand, we think recycled plastic is okay—we've done it ourselves. E-Bay has an entire universe of previously owned Legos, and our kids understand the concept that if something is reused, it doesn't have the same environmental impact…"

And so on. It went on to expound my somewhat confused views about war toys and weapon-play. But of course I never sent it. It just felt too, well, rude. Like, "thanks, but no thanks." God forbid I save the planet if it means being rude.

So I settle for a unilateral initiative and lay down the law for my own purchasing for our home, in which, after all, I often get to be "the decider." So, since the buck stops with me, I look at myself in the spotty bathroom mirror and decree: "Read my lips: no new plastics." And the sound of my voice does not echo off any mountaintops, and no bushes spontaneously combust, and no tablets are etched in stone. But the decree stands symbolically between me and temptation, in the form of tiny so-cheap-it's-practically-free crap. The crappiness of which is usually difficult to weigh against its potential for a child's pleasure, or an hour of quiet play in the backseat during a roadtrip.

As I shop for the kids' gifts, I realize how insidious the plastic is. The boys are growing out of the Simple Wooden Toys that are everywhere in this hippie town. I try turning away from the older kids shelves stocked with plastic toys and looking over in art supplies, where there are markers (made of plastic!), crayons (made of god only knows what), pencils (in plastic boxes, with a plastic sharpener), clay (made of plastic masquerading as clay), and a million other cool, plastic items. Costumes: all synthetic fabrics. Simple science project kits: plastic and more plastic. Board games: plastic, plastic, plastic. Mowgli wants a trumpet, but no amount of online searching will unearth a child version made of anything but, you guessed it: plastic.

I'm able to patch together a hodgepodge of acceptable items: previously owned Legos, cardboard giant blocks, a banjo, a chess set, puzzles, a rope ladder, and a grab bag of fun items from the hardware store, which does, I confess, include tape, which is not just plastic, but has who-knows-what toxic adhesives on it. And I also used the same type of tape to wrap the gifts in carefully saved paper from Christmases past before tying them up with salvaged ribbons. The Pragmatist adds in some wooden (if mass-produced in China and painted with god-knows-what toxic paint) festive nutcrackers, refusing to let my scrooginess completely rule the holiday. The family, not officially asked but also aware of our no-plastics theme, does their best, contributing art supplies (those plastic art kits filled with plastic items again), fun-shaped sticky notes (adhesive, again), and a number of stuffed animals (totally synthetic). But they tried, really they did. And they did succeed with several plastic-free(!) books. My mischievous sister adds some giant boxes of brand-new Legos to round out the mix and remind me what kids find the most exciting: big boxes of plastic, wrapped in brand-new paper with brand-new plastic bows on them. But I can't complain too much; after all, I'll be using that new paper for years to come.

january 1

The first day of the year seems like the right time to commit to carry my "no new plastics" resolution forward in a deeper way, by looking carefully at not only the items we buy, but the packaging they come in. There are actually many items I buy that I could be bringing home in reusable containers, if I just thought ahead. You can buy cooking oils, dishwashing soap, and tamari in bulk, as well as the nuts and grains I already get in the bulk section. Milk, cream, and half-and-half can all come home in reusable deposit bottles. But then there's the yogurt containers. Nothing but plastic on the yogurt shelf. The individual sized ones have already been banned, but what about the ever-growing, giant stack of quart-sized containers I already have accrued. Will it ever end? How hard can making yogurt be, anyhow?

As it turns out, not so hard. A quick Google search reveals a set of simple step-by-step instructions that only require I purchase a large pot that fits inside my stock pot, and a clip-on thermometer. The hardware store supplies both items, and

I'm in business, bringing home two half-gallons of whole milk (in returnable bottles, of course), and using the last remnants of purchased yogurt as my starter culture. All I have to do is sterilize the pot, create a double boiler, heat the milk to 185 degrees, then cool it to 110 degrees, add the culture, cover the pot and place it on a heating pad for seven hours or so. Energized by the turnover of the new year, I actually perform all of these steps correctly, and voila! Yogurt! Which I then pour into four of the old quart yogurt containers and stick in the fridge. My yogurt is a little more sour than our usual brand, but hey, isn't that what honey was made for? The Pragmatist rolls her eyes, but acknowledges that it's "not bad," as she mixes the yogurt into her granola the next morning.

Oh yeah! I'm doing a victory lap around the house. It's just the Ingalls family come home to roost around here now. What next, I wonder? Pig butchering? Maple sugaring? Well, we don't have any maple trees, but the boys are all psyched to make our own butter, empowered by a recent kindergarten shake-a-jar-of-cream-until-it-turns-into-butter experience. Next thing you know I'll be grating carrots to cook in the milk to color the butter yellow. I even have a butter mold around here somewhere (really, from my grandma, who most definitely did *not* make her own butter but who liked the idea of pretty molded pats of butter). Then again, with our pound-a-week butter consumption rate, that would be a lot of jar-shaking. And I seem to recall that Ma sets aside an entire day every week for churning. Looking at the calendar of the new year, I'm not sure if I have 52 spare days just for butter-churning. The yogurt, with the hot pad and then-leave-it-for-seven-hours instructions, practically made itself. Yogurt it is, a resolution I think I can keep.

This kind of cheerful, inspiring Susie Homemaker-goes-green story usually just irks me; I mean, who the hell has the energy to make their own yogurt, anyway? I tend to gripe: Don't you people have jobs? But I do have a job, AND I have successfully made my own yogurt, and it was simple enough (with the help of one of those turn-on-your-lights-while-you're-out-of-town timers that turns off the heating pad in the middle of the night) that I can see it as something I can manage to integrate into my life in an ongoing way. Don't you just hate me?

Don't worry, I won't rest on my yogurt-making laurels for long. Soon, I'll start to question my other dairy choices, and wonder what it would take to wean myself off all that plastic-wrapped cheese I buy. And the carbon cost of the milk transportation and the issue of whether eating cow products in the first place is adding too much methane to the atmosphere. I'll start to wonder if I've gone far enough, and whether if I really want yogurt and cheese, do I have to get up early every morning to milk goats fed from the native grasses in my own backyard? But for today, I'll try to stop the madness; I'll just stir some honey into my bowl, and wish myself a happy new year.

february

"Would you like tokens or credit for bringing your own bags today?" the perky, pierced cashier asks. There's a small cluster of people behind me in the 5:30 pm after-work checkout line, witnesses to either my generosity or my lack thereof. She may just as well have asked the underlying question: "Are you a Good Person, or are you such a selfish skinflint that you can't even give a few nickels to the needy even though you just spent an ungodly amount of your paycheck at this expensive natural-foods store?"

God forbid that hipster-cashier, I mean, Proud Team Member since 2007, should think I'm a Bad Person. "Tokens," I reply in a self-congratulatory tone. Double points for me today: I remembered my bags, so I'm saving the planet AND giving to charities.

"Meals on Wheels or Local Schools?"

"What?" I was so busy feeling righteous I almost missed the follow-up question.

She repeats the choices, which I translate to myself as "Feed the hungry old folks or provide opportunities for young minds?" So, I query myself, which one is more important to me? As a hospice nurse, I see firsthand how much those meal deliveries can help someone who can't really shop or cook for herself any longer, but as a mother of young children, I know how much the schools are struggling.

"Um, half and half, I guess?" I cop out of defining my values in the checkout line. I feel a strange sense of resentment that I've been asked to, as if I just can't make one more decision today, and they should know that and spare me the self-reflection. Can't I just swipe my credit card and call it a day?

It started out as such a simple request from an overstressed friend: could I drop by the store on my way home from work and pick up some cheese and crackers for our book club tonight? Sure, no big deal. Right?

First, I have to decide: which store? There's Discount Organics Chain (best prices, but jam-packed with overly processed and packaged items) or locally owned community-supporting Family Grocer (making their best effort to provide organic options), or there's Wholly Bourgeois (sure to have everything you could possibly need, including enlightened policies regarding food selection and worker treatment), or there's the Totally Righteous practically vegan super-groovy co-op, but that's a long drive out of the way. Wholly Bourgeois wins on geographical grounds, being the only one on the direct route home.

But once I'm inside, I'm skating down the frozen spirals of my own indecision into a frigid land where I must wrap myself in well-knit values in order to survive. I peer down into the cheese case, honing in on the soft cheeses I know my friend loves. I pick up a wedge of French brie, thinking that those French people, they're pretty careful about their food, they probably don't use hormones and all that in their cows. But I quickly return that one to the case: what am I thinking? That cheese was shipped at who knows what carbon-cost from halfway across the world. I live in a county filled with dairies. So, I think, I have to go local. And organic, of course. I flip over a cheese not much bigger than my toddler's fist to discover that it costs $15. I put it down: I can't afford a $15 cheese. It's ridiculous. I have two mortgages to pay.

But then again, it's really, really good cheese. And I did just work for eight hours, so it's not like I'm totally broke, at least in theory. And look at the other choices: what do I pick? Growth hormones, or trans-Atlantic shipping, or trucking from the mid-west, or cows fed hay and grain that may have been treated with chemical pesticides that are upsetting the whole ecosystem? Or should I go to goat cheese? Are goats somehow more eco? And how much do I like these friends, anyway? Do I like them $15 worth? Or am I afraid they might secretly judge me for making a cheaper choice? Am I trying to prove something, and if so what? Or am I just trying to figure out how to balance between what I think I ought to do and what I feel I can afford? I lay the perfect, doing-the-right-thing cheese tentatively in my basket, and head for the crackers, a faint pulsing pain starting to form behind my right eyeball.

Here in crackers it's all about the packaging. There's a lot of packaging. I get to skip the local hurdle since we don't have any local cracker producers that I know of. So I concentrate on taste and the amount of plastic in the wrappers until I suddenly have the revelation that I can skip the plastic altogether by substituting bread (bagged in paper) for the requested crackers.

Over in bread, it's local versus organic, whole grain versus white. I have to skip over one local bakery's offerings entirely, because their paper bags are made with plastic windows in them. I end up with a brick-heavy whole wheat seeded "baguette," organic and from only one county away. But I'm not sure if anyone will want to eat it. By now, my right temple has begun throbbing. Too many decisions. I rub it and squint as I head to the cash register.

I look around at the crowd of my fellow shoppers, and none of them seem quite as, well, neurotic as me. They are walking by the cheese case, grabbing a hunk or two of cheese, and then loading a package of crackers on top of the pile. No one else seems to be putting things in their cart, putting them back, holding two items in their hands as if comparing their literal weight would give a clue as to their moral heaviness. Really, is taking on all of this consideration of the upstream consequences of our purchases any way to live? I'm stressing myself out, and I'm not really much fun to be around. I certainly wouldn't want to go grocery shopping with myself. But if I give myself a break, what kind of a break is it, really, if it means another farm worker's kid gets cancer from pesticide exposure? If I'm not trying to make the right choices, I'm just pretending that I don't think they are important—I'm on some level denying my full humanity. If I am trying to make the right choices, I'm going both crazy and broke, roasting up skinny, $20 chickens. How is it we have built this kind of world, in which these choices even have to be made?

On the way to the chorus of beeping cash registers, headache following close behind, I fall prey to the temptation of the massive chocolate display. Chocolate or no chocolate, I sigh, and now my desire to do the Right Thing (which as this point has clearly shifted to getting out of the store without spending any more of the paycheck I haven't yet received) gets eclipsed by my desire for sugar, so I toss in a bar of fair-trade, no child-slave labor, even organic, but (for shame) wrapped-in-plastic chocolate, and then I settle in line to try and get home before the credit card bill does. As I watch the spiky-haired checkout girl scanning the purchases of the people ahead of me in line, I'm feeling mostly good about what's in my basket, as if the groceries are my heart made visible. But as my turn approaches, I haven't yet decided whether I'm the Good and Generous person who will save the chocolate bar to share with The Pragmatist, or the Greedy one who will eat it all up before I even get home.

And then… "Would you like tokens or credit for bringing your own bags today?" she innocently asks.

march

Some things are just meant to be. Or not. Case in point: the other day The Pragmatist and I were set up on a blind playdate with this really nice couple, the kind of people we automatically get along well with. We had so much in common, all of us lefty parents raising kids around the same age in the same eco-conscious community. Similar values, parenting styles, etc...the main difference between us simply the length of our hair. Of course, I disliked them instantly.

When we had finally escaped from their wool-carpeted, wooden-toy-strewn playroom, it took me a while to be able to articulate what it was about them that bothered me so much. After all, they were perfectly polite, nice people who served us organic fruit and crackers, provided our daughter with a non-plastic water bottle, and offered us all chemical-free sunscreen when the playdate finally went out into the yard. Finally, I came up with it. "They're just so *earnest*," I complained. What really bugged me about them was how hard they were trying to do everything right. They were learning Spanish so they could teach it to their kids. They tested their whole house for lead paint. They made sure their kids were dressed in only all-natural fibers. What bugged me was their belief that they could succeed at this, that there is such a thing as "right," and that they hadn't given up yet.

It was like looking in the mirror and seeing myself ten years younger, ten years more idealistic, ten years more certain, ten years less cynical, and probably fifteen years less tired. Ten years ago, we didn't have any kids, just a lot of theories based on the multitudinous judgments of the childless. The theories have fallen by the wayside and been picked up again over and over, and they now have the battered, time-worn appearance of almost everything else we own. The judgments have turned against us. Ten years ago, we thought we would raise our children to be perfectly happy, bilingual, non-violent, obedient, spotless prodigies-in-the-field-of-their-choice; they would *never* do whatever destructive, cacophonous, annoying thing that our friend's child happened to be doing at the time. Now, we settle for imperfectly happy, and we never say "never."

Of course, the joke's on me, that I should find cause for annoyance in earnestness. I am *nothing* if not earnest (most of the time). I try to rein myself in so that people won't find my serious-mindedness completely intolerable, but it's always there under the surface of pretended irony, my dire earnest self, waging my oxymoronic minivan-driven campaign for the salvation of the planet.

Maybe the real joke is on The Pragmatist, sticking around so far despite the fact that I've recently become *officially* No Fun To Be Married To. For my looming fortieth birthday, she offered to take me to Hawaii, and even before the simple and obvious equation of "two mortgages = no trips to tropical islands" sprung up, I was already fretting about the carbon emissions of the plane flight. How can I justify the jetfuel, just so I can be embraced by the volcano goddess and lie on a warm, perfect beach?

I *love* Hawaii, having been there just once after a lifetime of anti-island snobbery, the *Hawaii 5-0* reruns of my childhood and my grandmother's obsession with *Magnum P.I.* having stilted my sense of the island experience. Once I got there, I discovered that I *love* warm beaches. I love tropical sunshine and tropical rainstorms and tropical rainbows arching over wet, green tropical forests. I love plumeria blossoms, seeping their balmy fragrance into the tropical night air. But now, the sad truth is: as much as I would enjoy a tropical birthday, I'm just too *earnest*, and I wouldn't like myself in the morning.

What kind of freak says no to a trip to Hawaii on environmental grounds, I ask you? I think the technical term is "stick in the mud." I would say "party pooper" but then our two boys would whoop around the kitchen yelling over and over: "Mama said a bathroom word!" I've become the consummate party pooper, with my incessant yapping about compostable tableware and no-waste birthdays, my harping on thrift store re-use ethics and what car I should be driving.

At least I'm not alone—it seems everywhere I turn these days I get more news about the new austerity, information about the next thing I should give up for the good of the planet. Not just the luxuriously oversized car, but also hamburgers (methane-producing cows), bananas (carbon-intensive shipping), and so many other things. Making plans for a July Fourth getaway with friends last summer, our hostess mentioned that she has never been big on fireworks. Well, I'm certainly not one for rah-rah type patriotism, opting more for love of the freedom to dissent, but I'm a sucker for a fireworks display. The mass of ooohs and ahhhs and the pure theatricality of city-wide fire alerts get me every time. I tried to hide my crestfallen state at the thought of a fireworks-free Fourth and to casually (I hope) shrug it off, as my friend expounded, "I mean, beyond just the shipping from China, who knows what happens in those factories?" Great. I am now forever doomed to temper my enjoyment of roman candles and sparklers with imagined images of a browbeaten Chinese worker whose hand has been exploded to fringe in a fireworks-factory mishap.

I guess that's how all my friends feel after hanging around with me and my humorless eco-obsessions. Despite my frequent attempts to mask my many heartfelt opinions with clever repartee, my "good enough" buddy Selena recently introduced me to someone as "my friend Kenna—if you spend enough time around her you'll start to feel guilty for everything you do." Shit, and I thought my therapist was exaggerating when she warned me against turning into a fanatic. When she used that word, "fanatic," I had a vision of myself as a character in a Eudora Welty novel, hiking the back roads of society posting my "The End is Near" signs in hopes of converting all the non-believers. A caricature, howling into a sound-drowning wind.

Like that solitary evangelist, I just want to find a place of integrity, of true sustainability; but since I haven't dropped out of society, I find it inconvenient. Just like Al Gore said: plain old inconvenient. I earnestly try to put a good face on it, and so in my vehemence, I shift the burden of feeling inconvenienced onto the long-suffering Pragmatist. I buy cloth napkins, handkerchiefs, dish towels, and she acquiesces to these waste-preventing items. But then the laundry gets behind, and not having any paper napkins is inconvenient. And then we have houseguests, and not having any tissues is inconvenient for them, especially since our guest room is the dander capital of our house, being the favorite room of the cats. And then the oldest cat vomits on the floor, and we discover that not having any paper towels is inconvenient, to say the least ("disgusting" was, I think, The Pragmatist's actual word choice).

The problem with me and most of the other eco-wannabes I know is that in our damnable earnestness, we can't ever really listen to what anyone else is talking about. Why *wouldn't* anyone want to do the Right Thing? Why *wouldn't* you make that small sacrifice for, um, the survival of the human race, for instance? Hmmm, maybe you just don't get it? So we try to educate you, with graphs and scientific papers and explanations of projections and models. And of course everyone wants to do the Right Thing, but now all of our charts and patient explanations have backed you into a tight corner where you feel as if you have no free will, not to mention no fun. "How can I argue against the environment, for god's sake?!" you complain, guilt-ridden and resentful of the costs.

We keep thinking that if we explain how bad it is, how important it is, then people will just up and change. "Go green!" we cheerlead. And okay, maybe convincing people of the need for change may work in some cases, the ones who both need convincing and are ready to be convinced. But there are the rest of us, some not ready, some already convinced. And some like me, who couldn't watch *An Inconvenient Truth* past the first scene where Al shows the graph of global temperature records. Even having just seen the first ten minutes of the movie, I had nightmares for months. Al, as they say in Hollywood, "had me at hello." But I couldn't sit through the movie to find out what he says we should do to help, so I guess I need to give us all a break. Can I *really* blame anyone for wanting to blow her nose into a soft tissue that she can throw away, so she doesn't have to carry her snot around in her pocket all day?

Now the green movement is trying to get better at marketing, at insinuating itself into real-life human psychology in a way that doesn't turn people away. "Good luck with that," I earnestly urge. Finding the balance seems improbable, if not impossible. Not enough information, and it's easy to think there's no compelling reason to do anything. Too much information, and the scale of the problem pushes us past the point of despondence. Even someone as fervent as myself gets completely bogged down in the details and in the guilt of my inability to change as quickly or as much as I think I should.

So, after the kids are finally in bed, quiet if not fully asleep, I'll sit at the table talking, like a puppy worrying one of those "bones" made of a rope tied into knots, thinking that if I can just tease out enough of the strings, I'll be able to take it apart and experience the revelation of the magic answer. I'll figure out how to get to that Right Thing. Because the truth is, I do believe there is a Right Thing, and I haven't really given up yet. But like the puppy, all I manage to do is get more and more tangled up. The Pragmatist looks across our table and pauses from her late-home-from-work solitary supper to say with true feeling: "I'm sorry you have to live in that brain." And I look back at her, and earnestly reply, "I'm sorry you have to live *with* it. But hey, do you want me to dig through the laundry to see if I can find you a clean napkin?"

early april

It all begins and ends with laundry. Dishes, cooking, cleaning, none of it seems to bracket my days with the same insistence. Maybe it's the sheer volume of it, or the metastasizing way it colonizes every room in our house. Boulders of mud-crusted jeans and sweatshirts blocking the entryway. Pairs of tee-shirts and underwear thrown by the tub before the boys' bath last night. Damp towels crumpled by the back door, faintly smelling of wet dog and other things I don't want to think about. Socks and pajama tops hurled across our bedroom at midnight by The Pragmatist, temporarily transformed into a heat-enraged Amazon. A furtive pair of khakis lurking on the other side of the guest bed, shed in the early hours of yesterday when I'd come off a night shift and was hiding out for an elusive few hours of sleep.

Every room not otherwise accounted for receives the grace of Bright Eyes' presence. A week short of two, she still lacks the full range of words she needs and has to resort to other means of self-expression, the most creative of which is her constant fashion show. "I need a change!" she announces by pulling resolutely at her socks until they fly up off her toes. "I'm in charge of me," she insists, deftly wriggling herself out of a shirt. Like a tiny Theseus stalking a stuffed Minotaur, she unwinds her spool of clothing, leaving a trail from room to room, down hallways and back. Miniature socks collect in the corners with the dust bunnies, despite my near-constant picking up, bending over, picking up, bending… you get the drift. Mornings and evenings, I'm trudging through a swamp of filthy fabrics, or else wrestling through a mountain of not-yet-folded sheets and wrinkled pants in search of clean underwear. Sometimes I don't know how anything else ever gets done.

And yet, there's more to do. When I peer out from under the pile, the realities of this era start to stack up on my shoulders, even higher than the mound of laundry waiting by the washer: the climate is changing, the world heating up, the ozone disappearing, the oceans dying. From that perspective, my responsibilities appear larger than simply making sure the kids have clean jeans so they can go to school. Sure, school will help them prepare for the future, but only if there is a future. Probably every generation of parents fears that their children will inherit a changed and dangerous world, but my generation has more than just fear, we have scientific consensus. If I didn't have the laundry to anchor me down into the daily neediness of the household, I would be spending way too much time staring down the precipice of despair, frozen by my secret terror of what may come as the physical planet changes. Thinking about the giant piles of clothes that need sorting and folding can make me feel exhausted and sluggish, but my children's uncertain future, that's more a complete paralysis.

The thing is, I have no realistic idea of how to go about assuring a world that doesn't end up turning my children into extreme-weather survivalists, pointing their shotguns out the windows, fearful that any stranger may be coming to steal their limited supplies of water and food. Sure, I follow the "ten things you can do to save the planet" lists: I use recycled toilet paper, cloth diapers, compact fluorescent light bulbs. I don't give in when everyone complains that they like the soft toilet paper and bright light bulbs at Grandma's house better. I turn off the lights, turn down the thermostat, cut down on my driving, even as I despair in my knowledge that these efforts aren't nearly enough. I'm overwhelmed by motherhood, so trite in these times; I'm anxious and trying too hard to protect my kids from the psychological damage my parenting choices will inevitably inflict. It just feels like too much to have to save the planet, too, the added weight pressing me down into a slothful inaction, a high-fructose-corn-syrup-fed denial. But at night I dream of fear and loss, and I know I have to find a way to face my own role in planetary degradation.

The nightmares tell me that I can't NOT face it; but in the waking hours, I can't bear to face it all head on. Climate change is a problem so much bigger than me, I cannot imagine myself to have any power over it: I am a tiny dust-mote of a mother, impotently staring at an approaching hurricane. When I feel like this, I become incapable of movement. So instead I try to do something on a scale I can handle: I do the laundry. And when it is not raining or foggy (okay, so that's only half the year here where we have two seasons: wet & dry), I take the damp-pressed clothes out of the low-water-consumption front-loading washing machine and heft the basket onto my hip and out to the deck, where I hang them on a rigged-up system of laundry lines.

Thank goodness we don't have a homeowner's association in my sparsely populated neighborhood—our ragtag clothesline would surely be labeled as unsightly if my neighbors had to stare at it out their back windows. To me, though, it is beautiful, beautiful in the sense that when I catch sight of my laundry hanging out there in the sun, I am brushed by a sense of well-being and hope. Solar power in its most direct form—I even pretend to imagine my clothes soaking up some miniscule portion of the extra global warmth that's not supposed to be there.

That's when the sun is out. When the sun is going down and the fog is rolling in, it's more of a panic feeling: "Gotta get those in before they get damp all over again and then I can't put the next load up tomorrow and then the dirty laundry pile will get even bigger…" and so on. In theory, my clothesline is all good: good for my gas bills, good for the planet, even good for the clothes. In reality, it's a big pain in the ass. I get so tired of hearing "solar drying" advocates claiming that the sun and breeze give clothes a fresh-scented softness. Our clothes still smell like the residue of our unscented detergent, and they are stiff as cereal-box cardboard, not to mention the local fauna that come inside with each basket. When the rains finally started last fall and we got our first load of clothes out of the dryer, they felt almost impossibly soft. And there were no spiders in them.

Still, today another spring is poking up its shoots, and I find myself rehanging the storm-downed pulleys and wiping down the mildewed plastic-coated wire. And despite the fact that I know I will get tired of the endless cycle of hanging and taking down, tired of the complaints about the laundry taking too long and about the stiff clothes, tired of wondering if it really matters, I will bring the clothes out to dry in the sun all summer long. Last summer I got tired, too. (A middle-class, over-privileged kind of tired, I know, but tired nonetheless.) And then one day I was doing a particularly irksome load, a huge basket of almost nothing but socks, each requiring shaking out and its own clothespin, and I thought, "god, it's just one load, I could toss these in the dryer and be done with it, and what difference would it make?" But in an attempt to stave off my sense of despair and powerlessness, I hung up the socks, one by one. In return for this effort, the prayer-flag row of socks hanging on my line gave me a sense of hope, not a vague hope that humanity will sort itself out on a grand scale, but a specific and immediate hope that something I do, a choice I make today, may have repercussions somewhere down the line, the proverbial ripple effect.

The array of curved whites, blues, stripes, pinks, and seahorse patterns on the line gave me a sense of my own power in the face of great odds, my little David socks slinging their stones in the eye of the Goliath of global warming. The socks said to me: today you chose well. And perhaps this is what it will take, one load of laundry in the sun instead of the dryer, baby steps toward making the larger personal changes that will be required of us all. I looked at my socks, and I thought: this is it, this is the change, twenty-nine tiny things. They will add up. To a hundred tiny things. A million tiny things. And that became my mantra. A million tiny things. I will not despair, I will do a tiny thing that feels useless and unimportant, but I will have faith that there are enough of us out there doing them that they will add up to something meaningful.

A million tiny things. Sure, it smacks of the now-ridiculed Bush the First plan for social services: the "thousand points of light." But the thousand points of life were compelling, a beautifully indelible image, despite the politics surrounding them. They evoked the majesty of the night sky on a moonless night. They promised a simple panacea for complicated, pain-filled human stories. And the truth is, though inappropriate to carry the government's burden of social service provision, those thousand points of light still exist, multiplied exponentially—all the good people doing their good work, each following one call of conscience. My good work, my tiny thing for today will be to hang up the laundry and forgive myself for not being able to promise my children a certain kind of planet. My work today will be to see the massive anxiety paralyzing me, and to start to wiggle one toe. Just a tiny thing. And I know it's not enough, but at least I'm starting to move.

year three

We don't have to engage in grand, heroic actions to participate in the process of change. Small acts, when multiplied by millions of people, can transform the world.

Howard Zinn
A Power Governments Cannot Suppress

late april

The day after Bright Eyes turns two, I turn forty. For this mutual milestone, I throw us a joint birthday party, figuring it's my last chance to get away with the one-for-two party for a few decades. I tell people to bring no gifts except pies or something recycled. The morning of the party, panicked that my pie party will run short on pie, I run out to Wholly Bourgeois for an assortment of (vegan & nonvegan, organic) options. Turns out, my anxious purchases are wholly unnecessary: there is no shortage of pie.

I give myself a stern morning mini-lecture: "Okay, you're forty. You can no longer claim to be anything at all except a grown-up, and an officially middle-aged one at that. You are who you have made yourself to be, and who you are from here on out is solely up to you. Go forth and live the life you think you should be living, no more excuses. Enjoy." And then the pies start to arrive.

Feeling the full weight of my dual role as hostess as well as one of the birthday girls, I take it on as my personal responsibility to show my appreciation for each pie that comes in the door by having a slice. Apple, lemon meringue, and thanks to the season, an ample supply of strawberry-rhubarb (my very favorite!), one after another, whipped cream aplenty. And well after the point when I have reached a comfortable fullness, the double-chocolate-seven-layer-extra-rich-mousse pie arrives, and I find that even for me, the self-dubbed Pie Girl, there is a limit. Bright Eyes quit an hour ago, and even the boys are slowing down. I grind to a halt halfway through the mousse-mound on my plate.

But that day and throughout the week I enjoy the rare sense of feeling truly sated, that I have had as much as I want, that there is no hunger left in me. (The daily leftover-pie-for-breakfast doesn't hurt.) When my brother turned forty a few years back, I had been slightly annoyed by his self-satisfied speech about how he had everything he wanted: a family, a dog, a house in the city and a country place for camping. Yech, I thought at the time, having little patience for self-satisfaction in general, not to mention the natural sibling rivalry toward an older brother. Yet here I am, sated, feeling like the wife and three kids and dog and cat and suburban acre to play on are enough, more than enough. I am full of pie, and I have a good life.

A couple of weeks later, I notice that my skirts are all tight, and there is an unpleasantly distinctive abdominal bulge removing all sex appeal from my low-rider jeans. I decide that maybe turning forty isn't all flaky crust and sweet filling, perhaps there's a down side as well. I start to develop a theory that I have been harboring a time-release abdominal airbag which was set to go off immediately after my fourth decade; I look around me and notice that in fact, most women I see my age, especially those who have given birth, harbor at least a small roundness now. I've felt so ready for the credibility, the sense of empowerment that turning forty meant to me symbolically. But I'm not sure I'm ready for my actual physical body to get older. So I abandon my airbag theory and try to blame it on the pie.

Turns out, the source of the bulge isn't that important to me (yet). The bulge itself is just enough to reawaken my free-floating anxiety that had been temporarily stilled by my sense of pie-derived satiation. A rediscovered sense of my own mortality quickly buries itself under the more pressing questions of what I can wear each day without feeling fat, and how I can use my remaining days wisely to prevent my toddler from growing up into a dystopia of out-of-control global warming. Ah, the self satisfaction was nice while it lasted, but in the end, it doesn't really spur me on to action. So, once more, out of the pie pan, into the fire, I guess…

may

Newly two and independent of spirit, Bright Eyes shuns my offered hand as we climb the uneven dirt steps behind our house, old fallen leaves and errant woodchips piling up into tiny obstacles she prefers not to admit to. "My. Seff," she commands, teetering her weight forward to the next step, then tipping back almost too far. The pants leg she grabs onto as her rightful property is so perfectly placed to allow the rescue of her fragile balance, the preservation of her belief that she does not need her mother's help. After all, it's just a leg that happened to be on the right step at the right time. How could she ever see the careful application of patience, the conscious matching of her toddler pace as a gift? It is meant to be invisible.

I wonder about this unseen motherlove that brings forth a generosity and patience beyond my own understanding, and as I am starting to see my own face reflected in hers, I wonder about the similarity of spirit that seems to be emerging as well. I, too, have a great need to do it *myself*, to preserve my own sense of self-reliance even if it means turning a blind eye to all the props that have helped me stay the course. I start to wonder how often I have grabbed onto a pantsleg that just happened to be in the right place at the right time, and whether someone, something (somegod?) might have put it there on purpose. I wonder how often the sweetness of life has been handfed to me, when I thought I was discovering it on my own. I wonder if I might actually start going to church. But I'd have to actually believe in something to do that, right? And there's a part of me that thinks maybe I'm afraid to seek the comfort of belief because I'm afraid that if I give up my fear, I won't keep trying to fix things. So I just keep on hanging out the clothes on sunny Sunday mornings.

It's the right season for line drying: it's spring. So it feels okay to have warm days, until the heat wave strikes. And when the weather gets unseasonably, nerve-wrackingly hot, I start to really wish that I believed, not just in capital-g God, but even in the Rapture, the Christian biblical prediction that the end of life as we know it will come abruptly when the chosen are gathered up to heaven by Jesus to live in eternal bliss. Of course, the unchosen are pretty screwed, but who likes to think that they wouldn't make the team, especially when Jesus gets to choose? Jesus is a great guy, a forgiving I-love-everybody kind of guy, so he would surely overlook my human faults, blink at the list of my sins and my failure to practice his or any religion, and point his finger at me, the way no one ever did in picking grade school kickball teams.

If I could just believe in the Rapture, I wouldn't have to worry so much about the weather. I could embrace global warming as a sign that the endtime is drawing near. Raging tornados, melting glaciers, dirty bombs, suicide terrorist attacks—all would be perversely titillating in the global-chaos-will-precede-the ultimate-unearthly-orgasm sense: the destruction of the world as step toward union with God. Ah, well, I'd idly muse, sipping my teabag-brewed tea, it's out of my hands.

Even though I'm not a Rapture believer, I like them. "Way to adapt!" my internal voice cheers them on. And although I may not be one, I *have* met some of them, back in my younger days when I worked as a midwife to the Christian right, up on the border between Tennessee and Kentucky. Karen comes to mind, soft-spoken and soft around the edges, her carefully set hair rebelliously fuzzy by the end of the day. The fact that she hired me to catch her baby after my confession of failure to accept Jesus Christ as my one and only personal savior speaks to the lack of available midwives in the area during the early nineties. Her mildly drawled evangelisms couldn't penetrate my confused semi-intellectual objections, so she gave up trying to save me by the end of our first meeting. We settled for a respectful friendship rather than sisterhood in Christ, and she dropped the subject so entirely that I was completely thrown off by her shrieking in tongues as she pushed her baby out. Now that I think about it, I'd be willing to bet that Karen and her two sons with their classic Biblical names believe in the Rapture.

Karen is probably happily watching the changing weather patterns—the droughts, the hurricanes—with a contented smile as she imagines her children safely perched up in the heavens, clamoring for a spot close to Jesus to hear some parables. That kind of belief sounds so reassuring, so pleasant. Too bad for me. Despite my intermittent yearnings, I've never been able to force belief upon myself, warm and fuzzy as I imagine it might be. The end time, if there is to be one anytime soon, doesn't appear in my mind as an exciting event, but as a slow and brutal decline of human society, a violent competition for scarce resources. This pessimistic but persistent worldview of mine sends me scurrying for cover from the massive lumbering dread of how horrific my children's lives could be in such a world.

Denial is always my hiding place of first recourse. Maybe if I just go shopping and load up on eco-friendly fair-trade goods, I'll not only prevent environmental destruction but also prop up the global economy. Then in about a dozen years someone will have figured out how to fix the whole climate change thing and the kids will be able to get good jobs and have their own healthy kids and live a lifestyle just like mine only with new modern conveniences that I haven't dreamed of yet. Plus, of course, they'll have universal health care by then and the polar bears and penguins will recover, and it will all be OKAY forever. And to boot, I'll be able to spend a comfortable retirement spoiling my grandkids, in a secular, science-based "okay forever" kind of rapture.

The problem with my denial is that it breaks down at inopportune moments. I can go for days like: la la la la la, la la la la la, then… screeeech. Shit. Three a.m. and all three kids are asleep for once, but I can't settle down. Mad Max desert landscapes and ocean-flooded cities fill my liminal can't-sleep mind's view. Damn it, I need to call in the big guns. Only, I don't have any guns, or anyone to pray to, or even any Xanax, so I'm left with just one final line of defense: regular old human hope. Hard to come by in the three a.m. dark, but still, it's what's left.

So where can I dredge up some hope at this dark time of night, not even any moonlight reflecting through the insulated eco-model tubular skylight? I sure as hell don't want to get out from under the warm comforter to go looking in the back of the closet or the bowels of the internet. It's not there anyway. I just have to believe that there's reason to hope because I can remember feeling it when I was at the teahouse and reading the flyer about the veggie-oil bus that caravans up and down the coast planting fruit trees with schoolchildren. Those kids will be rad, eating their organic heirloom apples, right? What to me is an almost unimaginable, and definitely unbelievable, paradigm shift, will for them be a natural drift: "We *always* prioritize taking care of the planet, c'mon, Mom." A little child will lead us, the children are our future…middle of the night sleepless platitudes that nonetheless seed the desperately-needed hope with their grain of truth. The children *are* our future, if we have one.

This hope isn't quite as brittle as the denial, but it is fragile. Handle with care. Like the motley line of discount-grocery orchids on our kitchen windowsill, ragged pots tilting in old hummus containers, this rarified hope needs at least irregular attention. I nurture the hope with erratic gestures toward change, like my ritual of hanging clothes on the summer line instead of using the dryer. The orchids themselves frequently get dusty, our neglect of them apparent, but The Pragmatist always notices them in time to keep them alive with misty baths to which they seem indifferent until suddenly one day, from nowhere, there is a newly green tendril reaching up toward enlightenment. And when the small slit on the side of this tendril bursts forth into exotic variegations of pinks, I suspect that for the clutter on the kitchen counter below, unpaid bills, vitamin bottles, the current grocery list, and a soft half-stick of butter with a few impressions of the cat's tongue in it, there is a resurgence of hope, and even a whispered hint of a different kind of rapture.

Hey, I'll take a leg up wherever I can get it.

june

The relief of the end of school—the end of packing morning lunches, the end of being places on time five days a week—quickly fades as I once again prepare for the epic three-kids-to-one-mom plane trip to my parents' farm. During the few unscheduled days of packing, the kids thrash the house with incredible thoroughness, and instead of a last minute cleaning spree, I just walk out with the suitcases, backpacks, and the essential carry-on full of toys and plane snacks. I can do this because I know that the house will be clean, even sparkling, when I get back.

You're allowed to hate me. It's true, I have someone who cleans my house while I'm on vacation, or at work. She comes every week for three hours (unless she can't, since she's a single mom and things happen). In that amount of time, she accomplishes what would take me at least eight hours but probably more because I would get distracted by each piece of paper that needed to be moved so that the counter could be wiped down. Even worse, sometimes I'm not even at work;

since my work schedule is unstable, sometimes she is cleaning my house while I'm sitting with my laptop at the teahouse. Tsk tsk tsk, shake the accusing forefingers of my puritan ancestors, you lazy, lazy girl.

The Pragmatist and I came to terms with the idea of hiring a housecleaner before we even had kids, a time in my life during which I restrospectively remember having had all the time in the world. But we both worked full time and another couple whom we knew, similar to us in terms of economic status (which is to say, not the type of people who normally hire housecleaners) provided us with either sage advice or simple justification when they laughed at our surprise over their housecleaner-hiring extravagance, saying, "It's a lot cheaper than couple's counseling!"

Having someone else scrub our toilets was not something that we entered into without many discussions about class and privilege, about domestic economy, about the idea of "women's work" and how much less the housecleaners make per hour than we do. For now we've circumvented the issue of class by hiring a friend to clean for us and overpaying her. Carey wears hipper clothes than us, drives an arguably nicer car, and moves in our same social circles. Our domestic life is rendered immeasurably more pleasant by her ministrations. By mutual agreement, she takes on certain unpleasant tasks for cash payment, and we get to live in a home that at least once a week doesn't resemble a superfund site. Win-win, right?

Here's the rub—I've come to terms with the overall set-up, but there's a catch: I'm not only letting someone else take on the physical labor of vacuuming my floors, I'm letting her take on the weight of my own moral responsibility as well. When she started working for us, we told Carey that we don't use toxic cleaning products, only biodegradable, all-natural things like vinegar and elbow grease. At the time she simply nodded and smiled, but in retrospect I'm pretty sure she was thinking to herself; "yeah, of course, that's why your house is so dirty…" And since then it's not so much that Carey has gone against our wishes, it's more that she and The Pragmatist have established a winking set of secret signals about how much and when to sneak in some bleach.

Carey's miraculous white tornado efficiency comes at a price, but one that is easy for me to overlook. She brings her own supplies, including not only the superhero of vacuum cleaners but also one of those cleaning damp mop things that consists of bright purple cleaning fluid and disposable wipes. She gamely uses our concoction of diluted essential oils to scrub the mildew that colonizes the corners in the rainy season, but when I leave town, the tile and grout are always a lot shinier upon my return, a heavy dose of lavender scent masking the chlorine smell.

Eventually they confessed their conspiracy, and that's where I failed. I caved to their stealthy insistence that the whiteness produced by dousing our bathroom with a known endocrine disruptor is worth the health risks to not only my developing children but also to all the other life forms that encounter the bleach once it's washed from our drain down into our septic field. It's a strange set-up, a kind of mutual agreement that they will continue to be sneaky and I will continue to turn a blind eye so I can claim that my environmental correctness remains intact.

Once I face this quandary head on, I start noticing in how many other areas of my life I have cut these kind of don't-ask-don't-tell deals. And I see how frequently I'm content to let someone else do my dirty work for me. Like my holier-than-everyone insistence on avoiding supporting the sweatshop-fueled, pollution-creating, pesticide-laden (cotton), plastic-consuming fashion industry by wearing only hand-me-downs from friends and making all my clothing purchases at thrift stores. And perhaps my recycled clothing campaign would be a meaningful act, if only… I could resist my own urge to constantly update my wardrobe by procuring cooler, more recently hip second-hand clothes and giving the older ones to Goodwill. I mean, really, if my point is that clothing is a more durable good than the way we use it, and that the clothing industry is built on non-sustainable and unfair practices, then shouldn't I be making that point by actually wearing the clothes until they wear out? And shouldn't I be avoiding, rather than slavishly devoting myself to, the very excellent consignment store where the hipper-than-everyone sell their past-season clothes to the likes of me, since it can be surmised that they probably use the proceeds to further support that very fashion industry which I claim to eschew? Oh yeah, I know, I should probably unsubscribe from the thrift store Facebook updates. But not until after the next half-price sale—I could use some new shorts.

I usually forget about the necessity of shorts, living as I do in a place where it's basically never actually hot once you get in the shade, and even on arguably hot days the temperature drops precipitously the moment the sun sinks behind the trees. So in northern California, shorts are more of a luxury item, something fun to put on for a midday outing to the farmers market. Once the kids and I have arrived in Tennessee, my dearth of shorts seems like pure folly. The short skirts that make sense at home (because they're summery but you can always throw on a pair of tights underneath) just don't hack it here on the farm. For one thing, I need the fabric between my post-childbearing, post-pie thighs to soak up the sweat and prevent the awful chafing to which it leads. And for another, I'd just look silly tromping through the fields in my "town clothes," seed ticks creeping up my chigger-bitten legs.

Tromping is in fact my main activity here: to the creek and back, to the barn and back, up the trails leading each child in turn on the pony my parents generously keep for their grandchildren's use. As the morning heats up and I realize I'm only on trail ride number two, I search the scenery for distraction from my discomfort, and discover a pair of butter-yellow finches leading us along the fencerow, fluttering flirtaciously from post to post, keeping just one length ahead of us, until the fence ends abruptly and they dart off into a cedar tree growing where an older fence used to be. The difference between the old fencerow and the new one is stark, the old row a tangle of honeysuckle and other bushes, cedars and hackberries throwing a corridor of shade alongside, the new one clean metal mesh and sunbleached wooden posts, white electric tape along the top and a thin strip of bare brown dirt underneath. Inches from the bottom of the fence, a tangle of clover and fescue grass begins, carpeting the pasture. Occasional sprouts of poison ivy poke up through the shag, requiring constant maternal vigilance on behalf of the unshod.

But the almost uncrossable patch of poison ivy that bordered this pasture last year is gone, presumably the same way as the weeds that by all rights should be growing up along the fence. In my father's tool shed there is a space-age looking backpack-style plastic canister, with a hose and long nozzle attached, for which I cannot imagine any practical use except the targeted spraying of pesticides. I presume it gets regular use just prior to our annual visits, a grandfatherly hunt-and-destroy of poison ivy performed for the protection of my tender babes' skin. And I, loving so much the way my children run barefoot and free among these green fields, have never once brought it up to him or asked him not to spray the poison ivy from the pathways, even though in my mind I believe that the risk of poison ivy is less serious than the risk of pesticide exposure. His silent acceptance of this poisonous burden allows me to preserve a picture of how I want things to be when we vacation here: pretty and carefree and fun, like the bright finches.

A movement in the treeline above the creek catches my eye, and I call my little rider's attention to the wild turkey scuttering along the shadows. Mowgli is always more interested in the scenery than in the process of learning to actually control the pony, so we tromp on through the higher grass to follow it. The turkey is having none of this and disappears immediately, so my foray into the chigger-dense tall weeds seems for nothing until the little guy spies what seems almost certain to be the turkey's nest hidden in the underbrush, a wide low bowl of eggshell halves and fragments caught in circles of dried grass. Whether the eggs hatched out or were found by coyotes will remain a mystery, but the bug bites I will suffer that night will be worth it, for I have been reminded of my father's other gift to us all: the parts of the farm that he does not mow and spray, where wild birds and animals make their homes and continue to live despite all our intrusions. I am reminded that it's not black and white, that we can preserve even as we destroy, and that maybe as the generations pass, the balance between these things can be shifted. So maybe I let my father do too much dirty work for me, but hopefully, I won't be doing the same for my children, and on my watch, I'll let the new fence grow up with brush where yet another family of turkeys can make a nest, where the finches can swoop carelessly from sparkling sunlight into protective shade.

july

Back home in California, I once again discover a stack of junk mail and magazines that The Pragmatist has generously saved for me. The first night home, kids in bed early (love that time difference!), I pull out my favorite "magazine for thinking mothers" from the stack and retreat into the tub for my first bath in three weeks. And there, luxuriating in gallons of hot water, just hours after flying my family across the country in a fuel-heavy airplane, what do I learn? Apparently, my half-assed version of eco-mom is totally passé. So beware, the radical housewives are coming! Hide your secret consumer desires, guiltily stash your love of sleeping late, and throw the Netflix envelopes in the back of the closet. The righteous are upon us, proof positive that our failure to live a sustainable, non-consumerist, family-centered, carbon-neutral life is our own damn fault, the result of our laziness, greed, and general lack of enlightenment. Of course you haven't seen them, they aren't at the supermarket for you to run into. They aren't at soccer practice, or back-to-school night, though you might run into them at the library or the thrift store sometime. But mostly, they are at home, *not* out buying things like the rest of us. They are gardening, and milking the cow, and baking bread, and canning food for the winter.

The closest I got to canning this year was reading *Blueberries for Sal* to Bright Eyes and pointing to the final picture: "See, she's putting the blueberries in those jars so they will stay fresh for a long time and they can have them when no more blueberries are growing." Vicarious, fictional canning. There was a free canning workshop at our local hardware store (more evidence that the radical housewives are growing in numbers) last week but golldarn it, I had to work. Thank god, because if I'd gone then I would be suffocating under the weight of feeling that I should be canning these buckets of luscious ripe tomatoes that we are scrambling to eat as fast as we can.

And as it happens, I find myself without the time to do it. Which is the whole point, of course. If I stopped working then I would have more time and energy to devote to the sustainable practices of our family. I could break the cycle of work, no time to cook, eat out too often, get credit card bill, work more to pay credit card bill, etc. I could stop paying for *tae kwon do* and stop driving to little league games when it's time to be getting supper on the table. I would have time to build that chicken coop and get chickens and fix the fence so we could get goats and milk the goats and make cheese and pick more blackberries (if the goats didn't eat them) and can them for winter and grow a bigger garden and basically be perfect. And we would all live happily ever after (except without sushi). But I'm not sure how the mortgage would get paid without my paycheck.

Of course, we could just move farther away from everyone we know, sell the house and start over somewhere cheaper,

hopefully somewhere without little league because I don't
know any other way that I could explain the cruel and unusual
deprivation to The Percussionist, my passionate baseballophile.
We'd homeschool along with our like-minded, eco-living
neighbors and raise the leaders who will save this planet after
all and against all odds. Except, um, the market is down and
it's a pretty bad time to sell. Oh, and there's no way in hell I'll
ever drag The Pragmatist any father from a major urban area.
There's that.

The emergence of the radical housewives, not as solitary
semi-freaky anomalies, but as a nascent social movement, was
only a matter of time. Of course some of us are going to go
out and actually do what so many more of us sit around feeling
guilty about not doing. Guilty, but a little bit justified, since
it just seems so hard. And we're paying the mortgage, don't
forget about that.

Recently, my friend Susan, well familiar with my
environment-related neuroses, challenged me with the question:
so, what would eco-mom look like? If you were doing it the
way you really think you should be doing it, what would that
look like? Well, let me tell you, it looked pretty different than
the view I have in front of me. First of all, I decided right off
that eco-mom would have a lot more 1) energy and 2) patience
than I do. She would be able to include her small children
in family projects such as, say, building their own strawbale
and cob house, without chafing under the slow pace, losing
her temper at mishaps, or giving up in exasperation when the
first attempt collapses under its own weight. But it was a good
question to ask.

I decided that eco-mom would live off the grid, certainly,
but without giving up some modern conveniences. I allowed

her some solar panels, even a laptop & remote connection (outdated equipment, thrown away by someone else) so she can stay in touch with other like-minded folks. I gave her enough land to have livestock, because though ruminants aren't carbon-neutral, eco-mom could use all that handy fertilizer for her family-sustaining garden. Plus, she used their poop to create a kick-ass hot compost pile, which she cleverly built over a water storage tank: free hot water! Which of course she uses in her radiant heat floor as well as her shower. She has a horse or two she can ride from her farm to the nearest bus stop, conveniently located within walking distance of a local landowner's fallow field where she can leave the horses to mow & fertilize during her infrequent trips to town for library books and other items she can't produce herself. Hey, she's fictional, why not?

Eco-mom surprised me by turning her back on the bamboo floors and the hand-dyed play silks and the handcrafted, sustainably-harvested wooden toys and the organic cotton onesies. Turns out, hard as I've been working to pay for these exact seemingly righteous things, she doesn't find them important. Rather, she clothes her children in anything that fits, the more stains the better, whatever is at the bottom of the heap at the Salvation Army and about to go in the landfill. Same with the toys—she lets them pick up any ratty plastic playthings they find, the ones left in torn boxes on sidewalks after yard sales with "free" scrawled on the cardboard flap. Her children wear and play with, basically, garbage.

She figures that any use or pleasure they get out of something that has already been produced and would otherwise be trash is the ultimate energy savings. She looks at her yard full of faded, cracked toys and thinks about the Chinese workers who made them, the African country at war over the oil that shipped them to the U.S., the hard work that earned the money spent on them by the stranger's grandparents who purchased them for a child now probably in college, and she feels a great sense of connection, as if her act of eking out more life from these bits of junk honors all the people who worked and suffered them into her world. They will exist, in some form or another, for the billion years or so that it will take some bacteria to evolve to be able to digest plastic and break it down into organic matter. So she rejoices in giving them any use at all, and when her children tire of them, or they break beyond recognition, she presses them into the walls of the cobb shed she is building, as decoration, and as reminder of all the damage we don't know how to undo.

Eco-mom stares out from my imagination, begging the question: Why aren't I her? That seems to be forever haunting my days: Why don't I do it? Just because I'm in love with a partner who is, in turn, married to living connected to the grid? Probably not. Probably more like I've gotten a bit too comfortable in my armchair life of central heat and power steering, and the gap between what I think I should be doing and what I'm actually doing has become so wide that it now appears uncrossable. And then my good-enough-mom friend Selena comes along and shows me how much wider it is than I even thought.

Throughout this summer, Selena has seen me once too often typing at the teahouse and has now declared me officially "underemployed" (a byproduct of the prolonged Temporary Work Reduction at my hospice) and dragged me off to assist her in facilitating a series of community meetings about how healthcare can be generally improved in our county. The meetings have ranged from homeless folks at the food bank to powerful political action committee breakfasts, and the end result of observing the full range of local political power within such a short time is that I am feeling as though I have totally squandered the years since I graduated from college in pursuing self-fulfillment and personal growth, when I could have been climbing the ladders of power and broadening the sphere of my personal influence. Since that first liberal arts degree (Ivy League, no less, where one practically trips over the future leaders of the world—all you have to do to touch power is fling your drunken arms out as you stumble home late at night), I have, let's see, become a homebirth midwife through traditional apprenticeship requiring exactly zero college credits; spent a lot of time catching babies for hippies, Mennonites, and evangelical Christians; staffed various domestic violence hotlines & shelters; returned to a state school to gather yet another bachelor's degree (nursing this time); cleaned both dog kennels and horse stalls as a means of support; and managed to acquire three living children to whom I dedicate pretty much all my mental energy. Can you mutter "wasted potential" with me???

Sitting with Selena, quietly recording the opinions of those with political clout, I'm suddenly, painfully aware that *many of these people aren't all that bright.* And I've happily, lazily, given them the right to influence everything from who owns the local dump to how our water is distributed. And I'm brought back to a question I've been asking myself for a while: Is eco-mom an activist? Is she somehow either able to forego sleep and spend all night up writing letters to her senators, does she put the kids all on the bus to attend each week's various political rallies, or does she let the kids watch some PBS so she can make calls to Washington? Does she have time and energy, after canning all those organic homegrown veggies, to focus on the larger picture as well, or does the forest of asparagus she is nurturing in her side yard obscure the larger political landscape? I mean, are any of the radical housewives finding time to run for office?

I, for one, am keeping plenty busy just trying to do bare-minimum maintenance of my weed- & slug-overrun garden, keeping The Percussionist and Mowgli from dismantling everything in sight (including each other), and managing to get Bright Eyes down for the nap which is essential in preventing suppertime from being something other than one prolonged toddler meltdown. And on those rare occasions when there's a quiet moment, is it so wrong for me to practice baseball with The Percussionist rather than phoning Washington? It's summer, the sun is out, and no one home today can pitch a hittable ball except for me (and even mine are somewhat questionable). So we're sweaty and laughing together at my barely competent pitches, and no letters have gone out to my county supervisors outlining my opinions about local water policy. Staring after the ball as it wobbles across the unmown grass toward a wildly swinging wanna-be slugger, the wanna-be eco-mom asks again, is this really so wrong? Can't it be okay for me to be yodeling my excitement about my son's unlikely success at hitting the ball right back over my head? Or could I be, in the larger picture, striking out?

august

The school year approaches, and with it looms the end of the long summer days spent tossing balls, picnicking in the yard, and otherwise being at home. In other words: not driving. Once school starts, I will again not be able to hide from the minivan. So in hope of finding some way out of my constant conflict about driving the evil thing, I am spending these last days of summer in a serious flirtation with an electric car. Not just any electric car, but an electric car which is, in fact, not a car. I'd be the perfect target market for one of the sprouting-up Neighborhood Electric Vehicle dealers, but the current regulations for NEVs stipulate that they can't go faster than 25 miles per hour, and it's illegal to drive them on roads with speed limits over 35. That rules us out, as there's nowhere we could drive beyond our own street. So, the only electric car that could legally take us even as far as town, the ZAP car, is technically classed as a motorcycle, having only three wheels (which magically exempts it from the mph restrictions). And when you get in it, you feel about as safe as if you were in an aluminum can, sitting mid-lane in a bowling alley.

I would probably be more willing to let this very obvious safety issue override my desire to drive petroleum-free, if only our carpool wasn't falling apart. As long as we had the carpool, I felt at least a little bit justified in not cramming my three kids into a sardine can to get them around, but the carpool is just Not Working. The very exuberant neighbor kid Zach is a handful, my boys are each a handful, and when you try to put them all together in a confined space something happens very much like one of those chemistry experiments that the teacher performs on her desk the first day of class to pique the interest of the students: one of those stunts where you take two or three seemingly inert substances and combine them to form a sudden explosion of sound and noxious smoke. That's what our carpool had become by the end of last semester: day-in, day-out, ka-boom, cough, hack, "get me out of here!" Everyone – parents, kids, even teachers – suggested giving it a rest, but I insisted over and over that we don't have the luxury of being able to all drive our kids to school separately just because "they don't get along." I mean, really, can we fry the planet just to make our morning drive more pleasant? Seriously, now. My claims of moral superiority drowned out all objections through the spring, but facing yet another year of the carpool is more than any of us can really handle, so I'm test driving this unsteady, glorified tricycle to see if I can convince The Pragmatist that it's a reasonable purchase.

Of course, The Pragmatist has her eyes a bit more wide open to the fact that if I so much as sneeze while driving this "car," the integrity of my children's skulls could be severely compromised. So, a bit sadly, I leave it at the lot with the stereotypically seedy salesman, who couldn't even answer my very basic questions (you know, like about emerging battery technologies and the labor practices in the Chinese factory where the car was built). The Pragmatist, as usual, is probably right, even though it's very hard to walk away from a car that not only comes in zebra stripes, but also has an option for solar panels to be bolted onto the roof. I sneak one last glance at the bad-for-me but seductive e-car, and follow my wife home.

A few days later, school starts, and with it, my carpool-free, totally unsexy, nonelectrified life. Every morning, after the rush and stress of lunches and getting dressed and stop-playing-Legos-and-brush-your-teeth-NOW, I open the front door to the choices my world has to offer me: giant planet-killing minivan or tiny eco-sized "poor man's Prius," as I just learned my little Civic VX has been nicknamed by someone on the internet. So, no dilemma there, right? Simply, get in the little car and putt over to the school, using almost exactly half the gas I would in the big car. Um, unless. And except when. Unless I was up too much in the night and am too exhausted to deal with the whining and the "he's pushing" and the high-pitched toddler screech which translates as "he shoved my carseat over so he could reach in to buckle his seatbelt." And except when it's raining, since somehow the added bulk of the raincoats just makes the small car too darn small to squeeze into. When I do decree, "Little car today, guys," I am met with a three-part harmony of complaint: "why can't we take the big car, we like the big car, me HATE li-ul cah." I wearily explain once again that it's better for the planet, but I want to yell: "BECAUSE I LOVE YOU, DAMMIT! Now buckle up, or else."

The minivan is winning. It's like being married to a boring, unromantic rich guy: there are too many comforts to make it worth the effort to leave and pursue a more fulfilling dream. When we bought it, the salesman used a well-practiced pitch, repeating several times "driver controls all" as he demonstrated the various features. Windows, temperature in front and back, music, doors. Driver Controls All: it's a heady feeling for a parent to slide into the luxurious captain's chair, and for the duration of the drive, children securely buckled with at least two feet of airspace between each one, the illusion of control provides a sense of security generally lacking at all other times of day. It feels comfortable, insulated, safe.

It feels safe. Even though I know that our addiction to cars in general, and to unnecessarily carbon-spewing cars in particular, is making us, further down the road, not at all safe. Okay, I know that my car isn't the only thing causing global warming. The car is, however, the very concrete thing that I deal with every day that somehow sums up my failure to fix all the other things that I and mankind are doing wrong. But in any given day, my deluded driver-controls-all sense of dominion when driving the van makes me feel secure. Even if I can't seem to control my addiction to a car-centered lifestyle, or to the comfort of the captain's chairs.

So of course the minivan is winning. Especially since *someone* (who, me?) refuses to stock up on new plastic toys for the necessary entertainment of the restless crew, the minivan feels like a dire necessity if we are driving any distance over twenty miles. So for a road trip, down to the city to visit my brother, or up to the mountains so the kids can see what snow is, the minivan wins, neatly doubling the pollution footprint of each trip. Which more than doubles the guilt. But in the guilt versus comfort equation, the minivan keeps winning. Just this once, I tell myself, because I'm so very extraordinarily over-tired today, and if we're in the little car I'll end up yelling the whole time, a unending stream of "Leave-him/her-alone-keep-your-hands-to-yourself-I-mean-it."

One day I take the plunge and drive the kids down to the city in the little car. On the way back, I am so ragged from the constant intervention in backseat brawls that when Mowgli declares he has to "pee RIGHT NOW," I try to talk him out of it.

"You can hold it, we'll be home in less than half an hour" I cheerlead over and over, dreading the process of unbuckling and then repacking the sardine can of the backseat.

"NO I CAN'T!" he insists in increasingly shrill tones. "And I have to poo, too," he sniffs pitifully. Dammit, that rules out the straightforward option of pulling onto the shoulder, where the proximity of cars whizzing by at instant-death speeds would at least give me the excuse to insist sternly that the other two not undo their seatbelts no matter how much they want to.

I actually debate the merits of just letting him have an accident: most of the pee would be absorbed by his pants, not too much on the car, and we'd get home so much sooner than if I stopped. But then I decide that only a Really Mean Mom would make her kid pee on himself just because she is desperate to get home, and I'm not feeling quite that Really Mean this evening. And it so happens that we are near the exit for the town where I work, so I begrudgingly pull off the freeway and down a few blocks to my office, to which I conveniently have a key. Which is just as well, because by now, of course, everyone has to pee.

Already crabby from the previous hour of "can-you-please-work-it-out-back-there" wheedling and the fact that now bedtime will be even that much later than it should, I find myself literally barking when I notice The Percussionist absently pulling out paper towel after paper towel from the stainless steel wall fixture: "WHAT ARE YOU THINKING?!? THOSE ARE TREES!!!" He slinks back out of the bathroom, pursued by my shrill questions: "Why did you do that? Don't you know where paper towels come from? Why were you wasting those?"

"Look, Mama," Bright Eyes pipes in, drying her hands with toddler earnestness. "Jus' one."

"Good girl, that's right," I sigh, feeling guilty for my crazed eco-mom outburst. I walk Bright Eyes and Mowgli out into the hall where The Percussionist is slumped on a bench. "I'm sorry, Buddy. I know you know, and you were just spacing out 'cause you're tired. I'm really sorry. I'm tired too. Let's go home."

"Okay, mom." He unslumps and stands to head out to the car, but not without having to endure the commentary of the youngest: "I jus' used one!" The Percussionist rolls his eyes but is (thank goodness) too tired to start a bickerfest, and we manage to re-seatbelt without any bodily injuries. When I pull into our driveway at last, I park next to the minivan, resentment nudging its way past my all-encompassing exhaustion. "Why do you even have to be here, you big temptation? Why do I even have to know how easy it could be if I ignored the whole global warming thing?" I silently rage at its smug gold hulk.

So the days pass: Monday, guilt wins—little car. Tuesday, guilt. Wednesday, comfort wins—minivan! Thursday, guilt, on and on like that. And the minivan keeps winning, way more often than I like to admit, but I'm planning a counterattack. Maybe tomorrow, or next week, when I have a little more energy.

september

My fling with the solar-powered tin can car averted, I'm still stuck with a free-floating desire. I want…something. Something that will make me feel better. And despite the fact that I've carefully registered all the catalogs I used to receive at catalogchoice.org and they've slowly disappeared from my physical mailbox, I nevertheless am deluged with new things to want, things that might make me righteous at last. There's this new device that you attach to your exhaust pipe, and theoretically, it reduces your pollution by half, and there's some new kind of replacement you can make in your engine somewhere and it increases your efficiency dramatically, or there's this all-electric three-wheeled car (oh, never mind, that one was already vetoed). I want my actions to be more in line with my beliefs, and since I don't really want to change my behaviors all that much, I want one of these ideas that appears in my virtual mailbox to manifest itself into a realistic fix for the things that ail me: too much driving causing too much pollution and guilt. After all, I'm a middle-class American. Something is wrong, and I want to fix it. I want the product.

We all want the product to exist, the one that will make it all okay. Whether it is local produce, organic cotton sheets, solar panels, or a hybrid car, we want something, some *thing*, that can make us feel good about ourselves again. That can take away the fear of having to create a future we can't yet recognize, one we don't have a map for. Some thing that can make it okay for us to maintain (at least most of) the status quo. For me, it's the car. If I could just get back and forth to *tae kwon do*, preschool, little league, music lessons, and playdates in a (preferably air conditioned) vehicle that wasn't destroying the planet, then it would be okay that I go to *tae kwon do*, preschool, little league, music lessons and that I drive to work to pay for all of these things (and don't forget the mortgage) instead of staying home most days, showing my children the possibilities of a simpler, less hectic lifestyle.

I dream of this simple life, the kids and I all out in the garden. I used to love gardening, before I had kids. I went out at the crack of dawn to catch flea beetles and trap slugs. Now the garden is just one more thing I'm trying to fit in. I'm trying to add on, and I'm in denial that I need to subtract. I'm doing what I always did plus wash the diapers, hang the laundry on the line, seek out local sources for most of our food, join the green team at the kids' school, and put a home-cooked, locally-grown, organic meal on the table every night. If I just started with a blank slate, and added only the things that are most important to me, it would probably work. But as it is, I can't yet let go of the old life, so I'm trying to greenwash it, to lay a veneer of sustainability over my current lifestyle.

In classic American style, I find that underneath all my claims to know better, I actually believe that if we just spend enough, we can find that place of comfort both moral and physical. In service to this irrational belief of mine, we spend a ridiculous amount of money because we need a new mattress, the old futon having finally caused too many bedsore mornings.

"You know, *normal people* don't spend this much on mattresses," The Pragmatist points out, as we compare models in the Hemporium & Natural Bedding Shoppe. "*Normal people* go buy a very comfortable, inner-spring, back-supporting mattress from a *normal* mattress store."

"But we spend a third of our lives in bed," I begin, "and our little children with their vulnerable developing neurological systems sleep with us, and those 'normal' (insert annoying hand gesture for the quotes) mattresses are stuffed full of toxic materials and chemical flame retardants, never mind the massive amounts of pesticides used for the non-organic cotton, and the carbon cost of the shipping, and those mattresses are cheaper because you're not really paying the true cost of cleaning up all the pollution they cause..."

"God, enough already. Okay, okay, buy the mattress. How can I argue against *The Earth*?" she sighs, in a quickly-becoming-familiar refrain. "You win, the earth wins. I can't argue against the earth. We should probably just go home and make our own mattress out of corn husks."

But we aren't equipped, or perhaps just aren't willing, to make our own, so I proclaim that we are morally obligated to purchase a locally-made, all-organic mattress. So to pay for it, off I go to work another three 12-hour night shifts, after each of which I will be tired and clumsy, will probably break something and will even more probably take the kids out for burritos because I can't imagine trying to cook in my bleary-eyed state without creating a major fire hazard. Replacements for broken household items plus three family meals out equals one more eight-hour day shift. And on and on. But given how much my shoulders hurt these days, it seems that a truly comfortable mattress will be well worth the price of a few nights' sleep.

Maybe the new mattress, being so fantastically ecologically correct, will even help me sleep better. Maybe when I'm fully supported by my own purchased righteousness, I won't lie awake in the dark, pondering the million tiny decisions I have to make in the next few days, or worse, the big ones I need to make in the next few years. I can't even begin to calculate how many middle-of-the-night hours I have spent on the old lumpy futon, feeling trapped there by the fact that I should be sleeping, trying to figure out how to get rid of the minivan without ruining my marriage.

And apparently, I'm not the only one who thinks too much about these things. When I call my parents, my mother describes how, for a few months now, my father has been procrastinating buying a new car for her. Her old Camry is at the end of its useful life, and Mom wants a hybrid. It costs more, but they can afford it. Dad knows this, but like his daughter, he needs some time to figure out what is The Right Thing to Do. In what could have been a quite simple car-buying equation, he has inserted the variable of "what if we bought the standard version and sent the price difference in cash assistance to the starving people of Africa?" (You see, I come by my neuroses honestly.)

In this ongoing discussion, I come down firmly on the side of the hybrid car. My logic goes something like this: our purchasing power is one of the only ways that the Powers That Be actually listen to us and make changes to their choices, so by buying a hybrid car, my parents will be adding the weight of their vote to the balance in favor of newer, more sustainable technologies, and therefore, to our best chance of preventing catastrophic climate change which will cause starvation and suffering on a much larger scale than even that which currently exists in Africa. My father isn't at all convinced by this argument; to him, the hybrid represents middle-class self-indulgence, whereas sending cash to hungry people would be an alleviation of clear and present suffering.

As time passes, I realize that this isn't just a difference in opinion, it's a generational gap. He actually sees himself as someone with the power to create immediate change, albeit small; he views his world citizenship as his primary role. When I follow my own logic to its inevitable conclusion, I have to admit that at heart, I see myself just the way corporate America wants me to: as a consumer. It is only as a consumer that I perceive my own power. Once I frame the debate in this way, citizenship v. consumership, I'm almost convinced that he should skip the hybrid. But of course it's one thing to reframe a debate, and another to throw over core beliefs that have been seeping through the entirety of popular culture since my childhood. I still at heart believe that the hybrid is the way to go.

There's not really any way to weigh my father's do-good apples against my buy-good oranges, but it doesn't stop us from trying. We are ultimately attempting to answer the question: what can I, one tiny person among the millions on this planet, really *do*? I perceive myself as a force acting on the world, if only in minuscule ways, but a force nonetheless. My father's debate is really about which levers will be most effective in maximizing that force. My father scrimps and saves, does his own yardwork and buys his clothes at big box stores and his vegetables at the local chain supermarket, and he gives big chunks of cash to worthy charities at the end of each year. I have nothing left to give in my bank account come year's end, as I have applied any slack in the budget to upgrading the righteousness level of my daily purchases. So I do my shopping at stores that give better benefits to their employees, and source their goods more fairly, and I pay more. I buy organic food, considering the extra cost to be my donation to farmworker health, rather than saving money on this end just to send it later to organizations serving farmworkers' children who already have cancer from pesticide drift.

My mother manages to stay above the fray. Going more by intuition than by trying to follow my father's logic to its fickle conclusions, she has never wavered in her choice, and in the end she will get her hybrid car. Like me, my father will eventually let go of the debate and decide that, right or wrong, when it comes to cars, sometimes you just go with what your wife wants. As a result, he probably has lost some sleep, thinking about the starving African children. I tell him that in my consuming heart, I believe he's done the right thing for his own grandchildren, and for all the children of all continents, and for the earth. And really, as The Pragmatist would say, how *can* you argue against the earth? Maybe, just maybe, he'll buy my argument and sleep a little better.

october

The days have suddenly become noticeably shorter, but are still hot enough for me to get the laundry dried outside if I get it out there early enough. The leisurely pace of the summer line is slowly becoming a more pressured chore. But it has sustained me well through the summer, my clothesline-inspired "million tiny things" mantra, making me feel as though what I do manage to accomplish makes a difference, however small, drizzling hope around the borders of my days. An all-local, vegetarian meal here, a bag of loose tea there, a quart of homemade ice cream that prevented at least three driving trips to town for cones. My million tiny, insignificant, significant things.

Of course, once you start walking around your house chanting "a million tiny things" under your breath, it quickly morphs into a description of the actual tiny things under your feet, which at my house are inevitably Legos. Reused Legos from eBay (for the most part), but viciously sharp little bits of plastic, nonetheless. But that's the mother's lot, the masses of tiny details that make up our days, the reason why the small, limping steps feel like the only ones possible.

Unfortunately, as the darkness grows with each passing week, it seems to be obscuring some of my essential, desperate hopefulness. After all, my Pollyanna tiny things also have their obverse, their dark twin twice the size of Texas, floating somewhere in the middle of the Pacific Ocean: a million tiny things, probably much more than a million, all made of plastic. All these teeny tiny bits of plastic have found their way to each other, through tides and currents, to form a mass of flotsam so large that it defies imagining: a floating nation of miniscule garbage, just a small percentage of the things we threw away, the ones we let drop on the beach, or over the sides of our boats, churning into a new toxic continent. Unable to imagine how I can make a difference in the face of something so vast, I do the only thing I know to do to rescue myself – I head toward the washer with the latest load of filthy laundry.

Bright Eyes looks up with her irresistible shining eyes and newly minted words: "Let's play a game?" she hopefully inquires, squinting suspiciously at the laundry basket in my hands, "Yes, please?"

I stop to take a breath and reluctantly park the dirty clothes on a chair. "Okay, but I'll have to do some housework soon."

Her delighted run to the game shelf is my reward for remembering that housework is only part of the mothering gig, and I settle semi-contentedly on the floor for whatever dysfunctional toddler version of a game we are about to play. She pulls out a wooden puzzle, a map of the world, that I've always enjoyed. It's challenging enough not to be boring even for a five-year-old, but easy enough for a two-year-old to feel like she's helping. I like the idea of my children understanding from an early age that their home is just a tiny scrap of a much larger world. I happily worked this puzzle a zillion times with the boys, discussing various differences in geography and culture and pointing out the places Mama has traveled to and lived.

Today, looking at this puzzle again after a break of a few months, I'm seeing it with different, darker eyes: look, here's Afghanistan, where there's a war, oh, and here's the place in the Pacific Ocean where all the plastic is, and up here, this picture of a polar bear in the Arctic? He's doomed, by the way. There's a name for this, I recently learned: *Weltschmerz*, "world-pain." If you begin to identify with this word, it does not bode well for your state of mind. I sit on the floor with Bright Eyes, doing the puzzle, speaking the same sentences about the world that I spoke to the boys a few years, even a few months ago, but I no longer inhabit those sentences. I am pretending to sit on the floor, pretending to work a puzzle, pretending to tell stories about where her grandparents grew up, when really, I'm starting to spin down a dark tunnel of fear and anxiety.

I'm looking, quite literally, at the world, and seeing how tiny I am in it, tucked invisibly under a redwood tree representing the Pacific northwest. The sequoias may not survive increasingly dry summers; the young trees require more water than scientists predict will fall in coming years. I fit a panda over the rapidly coal-plant building country of China, not far from the Bengal tiger sitting atop the exploding industrialization of India, and wonder how we persist in holding onto these pictures of what the world we live in is like, how we continue to define our geography by spectacular, endangered flora and fauna. Shit, I think, somebody has to *do* something. And for my own sake, one of those somebodies has to be me, as the only corrective I know for anxiety is action.

But what to do? I always seem to experience paralysis from wanting so much, whatever I do, for it to be "right." The culture calls me to "Just do it." So, why don't I just get with the program and make the changes needed to mitigate my family's negative effects on the environment, and in doing so heal my own internal rifts? Well, there's my old friend denial, but there's also a much bigger demon to wrestle: uncertainty how to proceed, even when I'm trying my hardest to change. The denial and uncertainty feed each other well: if we're not sure what to do, then best not to think about it too much.

Sure, prescriptions for change abound: ten things YOU can do NOW to save the planet, twenty steps to a greener life, fifty ways to reduce your footprint, hundreds of them. But how it really goes is more like this: I finally get (almost) all the lightbulbs in our house changed over to compact fluorescents, but then another mom at my kids' school tries to explain some complicated electrical process by which those bulbs may be changing the frequency of the electrical current in my house, creating "electrical pollution" in the very building where my children play and eat and sleep, and then one of the bulbs breaks and I have no idea how to get rid of it since they have toxic mercury in them (but is it in the glass part that broke or in the plastic-encased "ballast" part? I wonder), and then I start reading more about LED lights and that seems like a better idea anyway since they are way more efficient and don't have the mercury (do they?) but I try to buy one at my local hardware store and they don't have any, so I go online to order one and holy cowpies, ONE bulb costs fifty bucks, who can afford that? But then that brings up the issue of how can we afford NOT to pay ourselves up to maximum efficiency—would we rather our kids live in a burning world?—and sure I could spend several hours online becoming an expert in CFLs and LEDs and EMFs and MAYBE then I would know what the right thing to do is, but it's time to fix our organic, local, plant-based dinner and there are ten thousand other topics that I need to research and get some expertise in to live this new green lifestyle and hey, didn't I *already* do the work on this one, buying all those compact fluorescents and installing them all over the house over the last few years? Isn't that what Al Gore told me to do? And, and, and… it rapidly gets overwhelming to the point of shutting down the hope required for action and sending me straight to the welcoming comfort of some organic but highly processed mac and cheese.

I look at my plate, and I look at the world, still partially constructed on the floor, but now with the ring-tailed lemur perching jauntily atop the redwood tree, and though I know that's not where that particular piece goes, in the larger picture there are a million other pieces that I don't know where to fit in. After supper, I'll help Bright Eyes put the rest of it together, moving that lemur over to Madagascar where he belongs. And I know I'm not doing it all right, but this is as right as I can get it for now.

november

"Mom! MOM!" Mowgli screams with an urgency and intensity rare to him. I instantly freeze and look up to where he is standing over the project I'm crouching to work on. "You're heating up the earth, Mom! You're melting the icebergs! The *icebergs* are melting, Mom."

I look dumbly down at the can of spray enamel I'm holding. This same son, in one of his frequent entrepreneurial moods, briefly took up decorating flowerpots to sell and use as gifts. Of course, being six, he didn't realize that the tempera paint he was using would wash away the first time the pot got wet. Of the many he produced, only one remains intact, the painting project having been replaced days later by a smashing project. This last pot is actually quite beautiful, a silvery gray interior with deep gradations of blue spilling down the outside. It surfaced as I cleaned off the workbench in the garage, and a few minutes later I happened upon the almost empty can of clear spray enamel. It seemed like kismet, the meeting of the flowerpot and the enamel, the chance to transform a surefire mess into an actually useful piece of kid art. I briefly consider the fluorocarbon issue as I lay out newspaper on which to spray, but I decide that since the spray can has already been purchased and exists, it may as well fulfill the purpose of preserving my kid's creative talents.

So here I am, caught in the act. And unsure which act I'm caught in is worse: the spray paint or the fact that my six-year old is this aware of environmental destruction. Don't get me wrong, I'm one of the most eco-obsessed people that I know, and I sure as heck intend to raise children who are not only well-versed in environmental issues but have a strong sense of responsibility for making sustainable life choices. But I also subscribe to the no-tragedies-before-fourth-grade theory of education, to let them develop a strong sense of their own agency and power to affect change before we throw the really big stuff at them. Big stuff like terrorism, violent crime, and the accelerating death of the planet.

"Oh, you're right, thanks for reminding me, I'll stop," I stutter to reassure him. I try to calm the surprise and anxiety out of my voice when I ask him, as if nonchalant about the whole thing, "Where did you learn that?"

"From the book, the penguin book, you know, with the penguins."

Ah, yes, the penguin book. The book that's been pushing all my anxiety pressure points. The award-winning, bestselling book that drove me to the brink of raving madness when the kids asked me to read it again, again, again, please, until The Pragmatist appeared at the door to the living room, a puzzled expression on her face, just checking in to make sure I was marginally sane. From her post at the sink washing dishes, even over the muffling sound of running water, she had heard my tone grow more and more shrill. She arrived just in time to see me slam it down on the coffee table and shriek, "NO MORE! I will NOT read that book again, ever." So much for trying to just pretend it was like any other library book and not make a big deal of it. I tried to save the evening by reading a thousand other books to them before they had to go to bed, but it was too late: the penguin book was indelibly printed in their minds as somehow Important.

The penguin book is ostensibly a book about math. A family receives a penguin in the mail every day starting on January first. As the weeks and months roll by, they need to decrease the ensuing chaos by organizing the penguins, placing them in rows and stacks and other sets involving simple multiplication. There are hilarious moments when the neighbors complain about the summertime stench, and when the daughter of the family loses it, proposing the simple solution of penguin stew. Honestly, I have no problem with math. Or with penguins, for that matter. What I have a problem with is the didactic yet absurd ending, in which the mystery of who is sending the penguins is resolved by an unannounced visit from the mother's brother, the "ecologist." He explains that the penguins' habitat is being destroyed by global warming and though it's illegal to transport endangered species, he escaped detection by mailing one penguin at a time to suburban America, all in service of his plot to save the penguins by eventually moving them to the North Pole. Huh???

Let me try and break down why this book sends me to the verge of hysteria. I'm okay with the suspension of disbelief involved in the colonization of a single-family home by hundreds of penguins. And though I wouldn't choose it, I'm okay with a passing reference to global warming; after all, it's the reality of my children's world. What irks me so much is the combination of the real scientific tragedy and the totally unreal solution. You can't just say, "So, since the planet is in a major crisis, we'll FedEx the wildlife to another country." Okay, maybe my boys are uniquely unsophisticated, but at six and seven they just don't have the critical skills to separate the scary truth from the frivolous fiction. Sure they know there's a difference between real and make believe, but not when it's all mixed up on the same page.

Perhaps I'm so triggered because the obviously impossible "solution" to the declining penguin habitat is a strangely exaggerated mirror of the irrational "good news" we're all counting on to rescue us. We humans also have a declining habitat, and we are rallying around recycling, canvas shopping bags, and compact fluorescent bulbs as if massive changes to the way society is structured aren't needed. We have created our own fictional, irrational solutions that make us feel better about the uncertain and frightening future. Maybe if we were just penguins, someone could simply find us a better home, one that we haven't destroyed yet.

Needless to say, the penguin book was "due" at the library very soon after we checked it out. For education about environmental destruction, we'll stick with Dr. Seuss' classic *The Lorax*. *The Lorax* is my kind of a book, laying it right out there with pictorial representation of a post-apocalyptic landscape on page one. Now then, shouldn't that be an anxiety trigger? Well, no, and not just because of the easy-going rhyme scheme. *The Lorax* tells the truth, using age-appropriate terms like "gluppity-glupp," about greed and over-utilization of finite resources and the interdependence of ecosystems and how bad it can really get, AND about what it will take to undo the harm that has been done.

The Lorax tells a story of bleakness and of hope, and wisely avoids drawing the picture of the forms that hope takes as it translates into action. The message, that the world's only chance for renewal is "someone like you" who "cares a whole awful lot," both calls the reader to step up and empowers her with the potential for infinite good work. The erstwhile greedy destroyer of the environment, the Onceler, places into a child's safekeeping the last seed of the Truffula trees which once formed the lynchpin of an entire ecosystem, the trees which have all been destroyed. One seed, one chance, bidding us to look honestly at even the meagerest resource that we have and figure out how to nurture it.

I'm sad that my child has learned that the icebergs are melting before he has had a chance to learn what an iceberg actually is. I've had to look carefully at how I communicate my values to him. I intend to impart them as guidelines for action, as my directions for making life's many choices, but I'm realizing that just as often, I show him the things important to me as templates for anxiety. "Paper comes from trees, don't use so much. Turn off the water, we'll deplete the aquifer. Close the fridge, you're wasting energy and that's bad for the earth." On and on.

Maybe a healthy dose of eco-anxiety is what's needed to keep us all on our toes and heading in the right direction in this era of rapid climate change, but I somehow feel that my six-year-old could easily be overwhelmed by fear and helplessness. For his sake and probably for mine as well, I must work harder to reframe the fear as hope: we can use less to help the earth, we can save energy, we can do *something*, even if as adults we know it's not enough. But we must believe that what we can do has meaning, like the child on the final page of *The Lorax*, reaching eagerly for his precious seed, and imagining a future that will only be possible if someone like him believes he can remake the world.

december

Christmas is coming, and it's summer this week. Seriously, shorts weather, and not just for that peculiar breed of northern Californians who have always worn shorts all year long. Bright Eyes is with The Pragmatist for the day, this being a day when I theoretically work, if there's work to be had. The Pragmatist sends me off to write, hoping it will calm me down (i.e. get off my eco-high horse) for a bit. After dropping the boys at school, I stop in town to run some errands, and while stopped on a corner with my fellow pedestrians, all waiting for "the walking man" to light up, we fall into the inevitable discussion of the notable weather. It starts with someone just remarking that it's nice to have a warm winter day like this, and someone else joking that with global warming, we might have lots of warm days like this. (*Yeah, funny,* I think, *very funny.*)

Someone else walks up and joins the group: "Unusual weather we're having." And that's when I reach my breaking point, and glumly reply, "There is no usual anymore."

"Oh, thanks, Mary Sunshine."

Clearly, time for an attitude adjustment.

An hour later, I'm breaking a sweat through my tissue-weight thrift store cutie-tee, as I hike the back trail at our local park. The winter sun shines warm and soft on my slowly-unstiffening back. My muscles like it, though it's a bit too warm for my taste. To stave off my fear-anxiety-depression spiral, I've headed out here to soak up some nature and walk myself out of my funk. I'm not sure it will work, since a big part of me would rather the weather was foggy with grey chill, seeing as how it's mid-December. Instead, I'm going farther and farther afield on this park trail, driven by the spring-like yellow light, searching for my lost sense of hopefulness.

I stop on a small wooden bridge, looking down into a darkly shadowed not-yet flowing seasonal creekbed, and am startled by a hawk flying up just past my sullen face. He seems equally surprised, each of us jolted out of our intended missions into a mutual paralysis of regarding each other, him as steady on his branch as I am on the sturdy bridge.

"Is she a threat?" he wonders.

"I won't hurt you," I silently reply, and he ruffles his feathers, settling down just a few feet from my marvel-filled eyes. I admire him until I am done, then walk away slowly. I am not cured of my anticipatory grief for the world, but I am less mired in it somehow. Today is simply a beautiful day, the hawk told me, don't throw it away.

I am wondering if I am able to take his advice when I pass by another hiker. She is almost past me when she exclaims aloud, "You have stars on your shoes!" Then, as if embarrassed, she picks up the pace and is behind me before I can think of a reply.

I look down, and indeed, I do have stars on my shoes. Big gold stars made out of layers of sequins, laid over the brown canvas of the sneakers, the kind of flamboyant fashion statement I rarely make. (I know, they sound ugly, but really, they're a hip kind of ugly, I swear.) These shoes were just my size and astoundingly comfortable at the thrift store half-price sale, and here they are on my feet, startling my fellow hiker with a kind of joyful wonderment, just as the hawk startled me. I look up at the welcoming sky, and feel the liveliness in my joints, and suddenly, I can see it. Maybe today is a foreshadowing of bad things to come, but in and of itself, it is simply a beautiful day, and the worst thing I could do would be to fail to enjoy each beautiful day that comes my way.

My friend Lotus, who encourages me to "focus on the positive," has recently explained to me that through her work in creating sustainable communities, she has come to understand how deeply, deeply broken the world is. "If you want information that would make you pessimistic, I've got it," she confesses, and then insists that optimism is still possible, as a conscious choice. And today I'm starting to get it: I can spread my dark cloud, or I can don my shorts and enjoy the weather—it's actually quite pleasant. I'm not hiding my head in the sand, nor denying the ominous portents this weather holds, but accepting its blessings nonetheless.

january

There are some things I do remember: "Twas brillig and the slithy toves/Did gyre and gimble in the wabe…" Not only the first several lines of "Jabberwocky," but the opening lines of *Beowulf*, the "Blow, winds, crack your cheeks, rage" speech from *King Lear*, even the full set of rules for who has right-of-way at a four-way stop—all of these have claimed permanent places in my brain. They all have one thing in common: I was under 30 when I learned them.

Bright Eyes' first word, spoken sometime between my 39th and 40th birthdays: gone. Was it "duck?" She loves ducks, probably "duck." No, maybe it was "cat," I have some bleary sense that she might have said "cat" precociously early. But wait, what about "Mama," hasn't she been saying "Mama" forever?

These things I will lose forever: the unreproducibly guttural chicken sound, the particular lilt with which she says "Dga-dey" for her brother, the upraised palms displaying their damp just-washedness. The loss of each new gain cuts at me a little, for this time I understand the loss to be irretrievable. Two never comes again, and tiring as two can be, there is pure magic in the explosion of language, magic I can glimpse in those brief moments between understanding and speech, magic that disappears as soon as I start to take it for granted, as I surely will.

If I will not have this juncture stored in my memory, then today, now, is my only chance to experience it. So instead of vowing to remember, I pledge to pay attention. If I can remember to.

The Percussionist has totally figured out the advantages of my failing memory, which seems to lose ground on a daily basis. I try to "outline consequences" for him (modern day parenting parlance for "making threats"), explaining that "when we get home…" or "next time…" and he defiantly giggles, "Except you'll forget, mom." "No, I won't!" I insist, but he and I both know that he is probably right.

Along with my increasingly poor memory, I'm starting to notice some other troubling trends. Like, I can't sleep very well. My nightmares about post-apocalyptic dystopias are increasing—I lie awake for hours wondering if I should buy a shotgun to protect my kids when society crumbles. I'm getting clumsy and sleepy in the afternoon, classic signs of fatigue. And one of the problems with being a hospice nurse is that you meet too many people who were feeling "just very tired," and then discovered an advanced cancer growing somewhere. So, I take my fatigue, and add in the fact that for a few months I've been having pain with ovulation and lots of premenstrual bloating, and *voila*! – ovarian cancer. The Pragmatist insists that rather than just complaining, I should actually go see my nurse practitioner, so under her watchful eye I call to make an appointment. I get the voicemail and start to outline my symptoms, ending up the list with "and so I was thinking that I have ovarian cancer but now that I've just heard myself say that, it's pretty clear that my problem is more, er, just, um, anxiety."

When I go in to see the N.P., she does order the ovarian cancer screening test, while making it quite clear to me that she is only doing that to relieve my hypochondriacal worry. I am so terribly embarrassed to be standing here half-naked in my stretched out tank top and least ragged panties (I hate those gowns and resolutely refuse to use them), a cliché of middle-class America, the forty-year old woman having a check-up because her anxiety is so out of control that her very young children tell her: "Write it down, mom. Now." (Usually in reference to some essential-to-them item to be picked up in the next grocery run.) I tell the N.P. about my environmental anxieties, and also about my terror of turning into the garbage-obsessed Andie MacDowell "Sex, Lies & Videotape" character, all of which she listens to patiently. This being northern California, she "prescribes" an herbal supplement for sleep and tells me to spend more time in nature.

The supplement helps just enough to make me realize that the scary part of my memory lapses have all been due to the sleeplessness. The anxiety, however, sticks around. If only I could dig up that climatologist/therapist, with his soothing "relax, breathe, recycle" mantra. I'm sure he would promise to spend his $120/hour fees buying only sustainable products in a way that supports our local economy and community. Yeah, but… although apparently I would gladly spend the greater part of a mortgage payment just for someone to tell me it's okay, there's no such person anywhere near my local Yellow Pages.

Unless… hmm, I wonder. And I call down to San Francisco to make a supper date with Kate.

Kate is one of those people who has not wasted her potential. Unlike me, minivanning back and forth from my suburban house to various suburban activities, Kate bikes from her apartment in the city to the farmer's market for her food. She takes mass transit to her office where she does things I don't even really understand, having to do with scientific global-level environmental policy-making. She flies around advising governments how to clean up their acts. If I think too much about it, I can really feel shitty about not being Kate. But she's so generously nonjudgmental, it's easy not to think too much about it and just enjoy her company.

After I show up at her apartment, we take her new Prius to the Indian restaurant she knows I'll love, and I start to spiral down, whining about how I think I should get a Prius and convert it to a plug-in (having spent way too much time on the internet researching the possibilities). She just glances over at me and says, with the full authority of her high-level understanding of transportation policies and air pollution, "But it doesn't make sense for you right now, with the three carseats." Kate, working as she does at a policy level, is not so taken with my neurotic, self-blaming theory of personal responsibility. She takes almost personal offense at the "inspiring" ads from Big Oil in which enlightened "normal people" models vow to "turn off more lights" and "use less gas" in order to do their part. (Thanks for the reminder, Big Oil. Sure, I'll buy your gas.) Holding the larger picture, in which there is adequate perspective to see that corporate- and government-level action is more essential than my clothesline, Kate advocates directing our energies toward systems-level change, rather than entirely dissipating ourselves into the infinite daily eco-tasks which can exhaust us. Ahh, the panacea of spending time with someone who actually knows what she's talking about, and is not lost in a bog of confusion and despair. Someone who takes a scientist's factual approach to the whole global catastrophic situation, and who still espouses doing what we can in the big picture, and hoping.

The evening with Kate, during which she variously disabuses me of the idea that I can purchase some internet product to make my car less polluting, introduces me to the wonders of the iPhone, and outpaces my neurotic worry with her informed optimism, sends me home with a new source of (hopefully renewable) energy for moving forward. If someone as informed, and as just plain smart as she is can look at the big picture on an almost daily basis without collapsing into despair, then there must be real hope for us all. So the next morning, when I notice that Bright Eyes' roses are blooming outside my window, three months early, I'm able to stop, breathe, and return to my "million tiny things" as a mantra of power, rather than helplessness. Systemic changes need pressure both from the top down and from the bottom up; since I'm pretty much on the floor, that's where I'll start: ground level. I pick up a thousand Legos off the floor, and then Bright Eyes and I fill some nursery pots with dirt. When the boys get home, we'll plant some seeds to set out on the kitchen windowsill, where they can soak up the light as the days lengthen until the seedlings are ready to plant in the spring garden. We'll talk about how we saved the seeds from our last year's garden, and how they'll grow into new vegetables for us to eat (if the gophers spare them), and how that will be a tiny, miraculous thing for us to remember our whole lives. Even if we sometimes forget.

february

About seven months after I have announced sadly but resolutely to my friend Susan that I am done with flying, that I will take no more non-family vacations that require me to board an airplane, that preservation of familial relationships is the only thing left essential enough to justify continuing to transport my body around by burning jetfuel, she sends me an email. An out-of-the-blue temptation that lodges itself under my skin, making me physically itch to board another plane, with no justification except my own pleasure.

Susan, my closest friend from college, one of my biggest supporters in all life ventures, the only person who truly seems to understand my Andie MacDowell obsession, is turning forty, and throwing a big party. In Brooklyn. Just the distance of a continental land mass away from my California home. Just a red-eye flight, just a weekend, barely 60 hours away from home. Just a break, a breather, a tiny sip of freedom from cooking and laundry and mama-uppy-read-to-me-can-I-help? Just a paradigm I'm trying to leave behind, but find intoxicating, addictive, and this time, irresistible. I reply:

Subject: carbon carbon carbon

Hey girl,

So, against my better environmental judgment, I'm looking at flights (and of course carbon offsets as well, not that I really believe in them). I really really want to come, and The Pragmatist says that if I don't I'm not only a Bad Friend, but a Scary Fundamentalist.

– k

Subject: have a place to stay

A's guest room is available, so I'm all taken care of in that respect. I'll let you know if my fundamentalism gives way to my desire to see you!

– k

Subject: I did it

I sold out to the Carbon Offset.

Can't WAIT to see you. Arrive Fri am by red-eye and leave early am Sun. Hope to grab at least a few minutes of real talking in there somewhere.

xo,

– k

Just this one last time, I bargain. I *swear* next time I'll take the train, better yet, next time I'll not go, have a lovely gift from a local-to-her artisan bike-delivered to her door. I could have gotten her something pretty nice for what I'm spending on the flight. The flight, and of course, the carbon offsets to match. And what does she get? One more face in the crowd at the party, one more demand upon her attention and time as she plays hostess to all and sundry.

Susan, of course, says that she gets more than just another body at the *soiree*, she gets a friend who is willing to compromise her passionately-held values to be with her when she turns over another decade. Susan promises to "compost up a storm" to help with the offsetting of my flight. She is trying to make me feel better, having received the series of emails from me, all dumped in her inbox at once, chronicling the torturous decision-making process that ended in my purchase of one round-trip ticket and the bargain carbon offset conveniently offered by the airline.

In theory, I don't believe in carbon offsets. The whole idea that I can contribute funds toward a solar project in Central America and that will make up for the fact that I am knowingly polluting the earth just seems bogus. Well, it's not entirely true that I don't believe in them. I do think that people and corporations who are dead-set in their determination to produce greenhouse gasses for their own recreation and profit should, since they won't change their minds, at least throw a bone to the planet by purchasing carbon offsets. Mainly, though, I've tended to look at carbon offsets as the modern day equivalent of medieval papal indulgences: a system for trading money for the right to sin without guilt or consequence. A lead-us-right-into-temptation kind of thing.

And this time, egged on by my longing for a weekend off, I fall for it. Click here to calculate the carbon footprint of your trip and pay your guilt-reduction fee. Enjoy your flight. The thing is, as I click it, I know I will. I will enjoy my flight, even though my brain will try and assert itself with the logical deduction that if my stated primary concern in life is preserving the planet for the next generation, I'm not doing a very good job. I will enjoy my flight, even if my seatmate is the unshowered, sweaty, nervous twitcher I rode with on a much-too-long flight to Peru in the innocent, pre-offset 1990s. I will enjoy it because it is not my job to bathe him, nor to assuage his anxiety. I may choose to offer him what solace I can find, but it will be a choice. I can just as well choose to open my laptop and work, or to relax into a novel until I'm drooling onto the little synthetic pillow jammed between my head and the cool, frost-flecked window. Twitcher-man can't touch my serenity, because I am child-free.

So, what, suddenly child-free trumps carbon-neutral? Well, just this once, I swear to myself.

––––––––––––

A few hours in the air, and by Saturday night I am happily ensconced in the white corner of an all-white room, sipping wine, nibbling meatballs served on the ends of long skewers, chatting almost frantically with an ever-shifting array of old friends and acquaintances. The alcohol, the company, the mere over-educated, black-clad homogeneity of the small group of people in the room all make me feel safer than I've felt in a long time. I want to stay here forever, among this collection of self-admittedly smart, thinking people who are living as if life were stable, moving forward with deciding where to send their children to school, attending cocktail parties while friendly college students watch over their sleeping children. Hours slip by unnoticed, and my confessions of obsessive environment-related anxieties become ever-more far removed from the immediate reality of friendship, intellectual stimulation, and carefully chosen hors-d'oeuvres. I came to the party expecting to turn in early, and I'm the last to notice that the party is officially over and now moving caterpillar-like across the street to a late-night bar. I am, against my instinct, just plain having fun.

At the bar, yet another old college friend sidles up to remark on my adventurous, non-New York lifestyle. Over his hipper-than-thou art critic's glasses, he peers earnestly at me and notes: "You're probably the only one of us with any skills which will be useful when it all ends," as if we can all take for granted that it will end, this endless cocktail party of globalization and expanding consumerism. And I have to agree, that if we all end up trying to live off the land, my experience as a homebirth midwife will likely be much handier than an illustrious publishing record, or an impressive teaching fellowship. But for tonight, the after-party is still in full swing, and we are all a bit tipsy by this time, and it seems a bit improbable, and definitely distant, this potential need for "real" skills.

On the way home, too early the next morning, I sleepily skim through a *New Yorker* magazine jettisoned by a fellow traveler, and read a long profile of a lifeboat-living (literally, for him, a boat) intelligent, articulate social analyst who is simply rationally preparing for the imminent full collapse of society as we know it. I can't read the full profile, moving after the first few paragraphs to skimming, then giving up altogether. All it's doing is reminding me of something that I already know deep inside, that we have to remake the world, and that I'm not doing so well at my part of it. I peer out the plexiglass windows at the airplane wings, taking in the snow-covered expanses of America passing below me. The snow provides a veneer of comfort (Look, it's cold!) but nevertheless, I wonder again how it is that I am living a life so far from what seems rational at this point, given that I actually believe it all.

Fortunately, the same *New Yorker* contains an analysis of the American health care system, providing a convincing argument that any wholesale change to an existing system has to come about organically, using existing structures and patterns to move to the next step. That's more like it. Healthcare, energy use, agricultural policy, climate agreements—there's so much change needed. We can't all just all opt out, throw off our lives and move onto well-stocked lifeboats; but here's someone arguing that we can change systems over time, one vote, one action at a time, until the whole is transformed.

Sitting on this claustrophobic, carbon-spewing plane, but still under the influence of both the wine and the happiness of the night before, I wonder which way the balance will tip. Will we pull it off? In time, will our desire for change translate into an electric, functional high-speed train system? I hope so, but I am afraid of the possibility that we will settle for not enough, that our desire for change will derail, that the availability of a carbon offset with one extra mouse-click will change us. Please, I pray, as the plane hits a stretch of turbulence that bounces the magazine out of my limpid, half-asleep hands, please, let us get there safely.

march

The lifeboat is pulling me under. There is no buoyancy to it, at least, not for me. I am not on the lifeboat. I am floating farther and farther from the sinking ship, desperately clinging to some swiftly waterlogging flotsam. In this stubbornly recurring nightmare, the lifeboat is within sight but out of reach, and knowing that it's there, and that I'm not on it, makes my drenched clothing pull me down that much faster.

Ever since a friend told me about her lifeboat, in a kind of embarrassed way, it has been haunting my bedroom on random nights. It sneaks out from under the bed after I've finally dozed off, and whispers an icy "Boo!" in my ear, so that I'm trapped awake, knowing that it's not some immediate threat I'm hearing, but a whiff of a possible future, one in which not only I but also my children are drowning, because we weren't on the lifeboat. I lie awake for an eternity, until the grey seeps into the (electricity-saving) skylight.

In the bright morning, I yell at the kids for the most minor infractions of the these-tasks-must be-done-in-a-timely-manner

before-school routine, simply because I am both exhausted and
jacked up on anxiety.

Then I take a deep breath and in a trembly voice try to
explain, "Hey guys, Mama's kind of not feeling so great right
now, kind of scared and so I'm not dealing very well when you
aren't doing what you need to do. I'm sorry, I shouldn't yell, but
can you all help by just trying a little harder to get ready?"

They immediately hone in on the most truthful part of my
monologue, and gather around curiously. "Why are you scared,
Mama? What are you scared of?"

Oh, shit. I'm a worse mom that I thought. Now I've not
only yelled at them for no reason, I've freaked them out.

"Um, guys, it's not like I'm really scared of something real,
just sometimes I get scared that I won't always be able to take
care of you, or that people won't be nice." Kind of honest,
but super-lame. "But you know, and I know, that today I *can*
take care of you, and we live around a lot of really nice people,
right?" Backpedal, backpedal. "So, um. Guys, let's all just try to
be nice to each other right now, and I'll try harder too, okay?"

"Whatever, Mom." Okay, so they don't really say it, but it's
all over their faces.

We make it out into the much, much too warm early March
morning, crammed into the little car today, which should make
me feel better, except I can't stop thinking about the lifeboat.
I brood silently throughout the drive to their school, ignoring
the discontented rabble in the back seat.

The "lifeboat" is a concept that immediately made sense
to me, a place set up to be isolated and self-sustaining in the
case of probable food shortages and possible massive social
unrest resulting from climate changes. My friend's lifeboat
is a hundred acres well off the beaten track, where they are

presumably setting up a solar well pump and building shelters and storing seeds and suchlike survivalist activities. They have a group of people all working on it together, planting orchards and I don't know what else. And in case you are picturing neo-luddite survivalist types, let me correct you—these are perfectly normal, actually more normal than me (in a less-likely-to-prepare-for-armageddon way) folks, urban hipsters toting the latest e-gadgets, the latest fashions.

Actually, I don't know many of the details. That first conversation with my friend was awkward, sheepish on both sides, and since then I've been so tortured by the whole thing that I'm terrified to bring it up again. The only detail I remember distinctly was that she happened to throw in, "Apparently, so many people are doing this that it's become difficult to order bulk fruit trees, they're all sold out."

So many people? So many people can afford to maintain their regular life and on the side buy a big farm somewhere to set up a just-in-case homestead? Am I so much of a loser that I'm among the few who haven't amassed that kind of wealth, or at least the kind of friends that would invite me along? And beyond that, "so many people" believe that it's all going to get that bad, that the chaos is inevitable, and so the best place to put their energy is into an escape route?

Maybe I should just climb onto the lifeboat, and sleep easy from the hard work of planting orchards and the comforting knowledge that I've done all I can. Easy enough, right? Except for one thing: I wasn't invited to the lifeboat. Which means I'm not even sure if my distress is caused more by the threat of an uncertain future, or by a leftover pre-adolescent longing to belong, to be included.

It's not like we're poor. We could do it too, if that's what we chose to do. We could sell our house and move somewhere less ridiculously overpriced and build a cobb house and live off the grid with minimal inputs from the outside world. We could walk away from the community we have, the little league games, the mortgages and the need to pay them, and make our main work the feeding of our family. We could, but we won't. There's the first issue, that if this were the life choice I decided was right for me, there wouldn't be a "we" anymore. There would be a "me," divorced and lonely out there tending the orchard, once I was able to get my hands on some trees to plant. And then there's the more philosophical issue, the scarier thing to ask: what's the right thing to do? Scary, because the more I ask it, the less I know the answer.

At first, I just take the self-justifying route of claiming that the right place to invest our energies is into our communities, into not just our own survival but the survival of our neighbors, our cities, our world. If we're going to spend a bunch of time and energy preparing for global warming, doesn't it make sense to put that time and energy into projects that help everyone, not just a select few? I can already hear the soft whine of judgment sneaking into my voice. But seriously, how would we decide who gets to come on the lifeboat?

Of course, in a way it's easy—you just collect some friends and family, particularly those with skills transferable to a subsistence economy, and you get with the business of ensuring the survival of your progeny, to the best of your ability. But doesn't it start to feel a little uncomfortably elitist, the notion of determining the deserving and the un-deserving, when you look at it from a little bit of distance? Like, why doesn't the annoying neighbor get to come? Well, yes, she's prone to demanding that we clean her gutters during rainstorms because the leaves from our tree are blocking them, but does that mean we just cut her off, slap her grasping hands away from the boat since there's not enough room for everyone? Just because we don't *like* her?

When we get to the school, I pull it together for long enough to navigate the complicated drop-off process. Thanks to my yelling, we've arrived early enough to claim one of the actual parking spots in the gravel loop that serves as driveway, parking lot, walking path, and drainage ditch for our budget-challenged institution. The kids squeeze out of the back seat circus-clown style, half-heeding my admonitions to "stay together, please, watch the cars, don't let your sister get ahead!" while I fish the lunches out of the front passenger footwell and scurry to catch up, trying at least to look like a good mom who doesn't let her children get run over by a blind-backing minivan.

The Percussionist hugs me goodbye with a show of first-grade reluctance before trotting off to the field where his class runs a morning lap. Then Bright Eyes starts begging me to push her on the big kid swings while I try to coax Mowgli into a non-coerced nature walk in the fifteen minutes we have before kindergarten drop-off time. The nature walk is supposed to help him ground himself to enter the classroom calmly. And no wonder that he would need such a thing, with an insomniac mother hounding him to "HURRY UP NOW!" until he's out of the house.

This morning it works like it's supposed to: he doesn't fight the walk, Bright Eyes tags along cheerfully. Mowgli slips into his class just as the first song is beginning. Bright Eyes contents herself with a few minutes on the monkey bars while I catch up with some of the other moms in this close-knit school community. One of them is starting a school foodbank to help the families who are struggling, and I become a bit red-eyed, feeling like there's so much to lose if we ever really walked away from all this. Soon the moms scatter, off to various jobs and errands. I plan to detour from my usual route home so I can stop by the teahouse and use their wireless connection to fire off some seemingly urgent email.

Starting the car restarts my previous line of thoughts as well, but in this moment I'm feeling more sure of my position. No lifeboat. All for one and one for all. Take the moral high road. But, as I get farther from the schoolyard, doubt creeps back in...is the moral high road going to make me feel better if it all goes to hell? Am I sacrificing my children to some ill-defined so-called values? Do the people on the lifeboat love their children more than I do? These questions smother me, pinning my mind down in an unnavigable darkness, unable to see or move, as I drive into town on autopilot. I am terrified that all this waking self does, all the sending of urgent emails and shopping for food and paying of bills and driving to *tae kwon do* (carpooling, yes, but still driving) is really just me desperately dancing to the band as they play on ever more insistently, despite the rising water and the tilting floor.

At the teahouse, I buy some screen time with a pot of (organic) herbal tea and various containers of ice cubes, (organic) milk, and honey crystals with which Bright Eyes can conduct toddler-sized chemistry experiments. And despite the distressingly pleasant weather and my insomniac hangover, today is my lucky day, because Selena's good-enough husband walks in.

I slather him with my pent-up anxiety, and he laughs without malice. As I'm yammering on about the lack of rainfall, he reminds me that there are some permaculture folks doing interesting things in climates with much less rain than our own. His tea arrives at the table where he's set down his stuff, and he goes to drink it, leaving me with my laptop and my circular thoughts. I've been obsessing that our one acre isn't enough land to support us, but now I have a new mantra for the day: permaculture. Permaculture. Ah, so soothing. Living roofs and water recycling methods. Designs for living in harmony with natural eco-systems. "Permaculture" will get me through the next several hours while I go about the daily care and feeding of my family, until I can pass out while cuddling one of the kids to sleep. There's just nothing about the word "permaculture" not to love, with its connotation of durable livability set against an uncertain future.

My town is a hotbed of permaculture activism and post-carbon visionaries (okay, yes, and pot-growing hippies). So, with my new mantra, my to-do list has changed, from wondering if we should build a lifeboat to realizing that I might well already be in one, this town where people are tearing down the fences between their back yards and installing sprawling food gardens. It's not isolated and defensible and organized, but I'll throw my lot in with it, as it contains so many people whom I love. Well-intentioned, doing-the-best-we-can people.

People in my community are struggling and failing and hurting each other and ourselves, just like everywhere, but we are also creating and supporting an astounding number of small organic farms. Our town mascot, you might call him, is a folk artist who builds oversized, loudly colored replicas of the local residents out of junk. We allow our haphazard but well-intentioned "sculpture jam" creations a public venue. We may be elitist in our trying-so-hard, organic, homegrown righteous way, in our "local flavor, global vision" town brand (Really! It's supposed to attract eco-tourists.), but check out our public art, and you'll see, at heart we're not even the least bit pretentious.

Walk by any bulletin board in this town, and you'll see, among the posters for the local bands, flyers for sound healing, energy healing, healing breath, healing through movement, transformational healing. We are clearly a people who have admitted our brokenness. And to me, all these different people yearning toward wholeness can at times seem slightly ridiculous, but when I drop my own pretensions, then I can see them as part of the whole, as part of something larger than any one of us, and I'm glad they're all here, urging the healing of the world.

As Selena's husband prepares to move on with his day, I notice that he's carrying a plastic bag full of what appear to be sticks. I shoot him a questioning glance, and he comes back over to explain that he just came from a rare-fruit grower's exchange, where (for free!) he has collected a wide variety of different strains of apples and plums to graft onto any existing apple or plum tree, creating backyard biodiversity on a microcosmic scale. He must have seen the gleam of covetousness in my eye, for he offered: "They'll give you some anytime, they want to give them away, so we can have all different kinds of fruit growing at once, everywhere."

So, this is my town, and here we are, probably to stay. Perhaps I could do more to love my children, perhaps I'm risking them by failing to secure them the necessary acreage to grow all their food, but at least I won't have to explain to them why we left the neighbors behind. And while we wait for the iceberg to hit, or, more scientifically, to finish melting, I'll see what plans the permaculture folks can help me dream up for one well-intentioned if occasionally insomniac acre of dry land. It even looks like I might be able to rustle up some fruit trees.

april

Our birthdays are upon us again, and this time, Bright Eyes is having no part of the Mama-and-me party. She wants "my own pink birt-day," replete with "hot dogs, salalad, sweet po-matos, and pink cake." That's a girl who knows her own mind.

Pink cake should not be too much of a problem, really. After all, the bakery cases are full of them. The problem is, we have a family tradition of making our own cakes, and I'm not much of a baker. The Percussionist laid the groundwork for this, since he actually doesn't like cake, but always wants to have a birthday "cake" for his party. So I've become adept at producing cake-like creations made entirely from ice cream. Mowgli wants at least one layer of his cakes to be ice cream, and usually has some strangely specific request for the other layer, such as banana bread, or zucchini cake, that makes it easy to pull out a recipe and fake it. But Bright Eyes wants an all-cake pink cake, and (since I'm trying to protect her little ovaries from synthetic red dye) it proves to be out of my league.

I think I'm okay, because I have an until-now foolproof recipe for basic yellow cake, which is the only cake I've ever been able to make that wasn't dry and crumbly. So the morning of the party, we get out the idiosyncratic but still functional mixer, and start mixing up the yellow cake. Bright Eyes gamely wields the potato masher in a bowl of sliced ripe strawberries and drops handfuls of the resultant mush into the spinning bowl of batter, turning it an ever-so-slight shade of pink. But the delight in her face at this moment is worth all the disaster the cake will turn out to be, because she is clapping and jumping up and down on the chair I have pushed up to the counter for her: "Pink, pink! My cake is pink!" I take one more look at the barely good-enough yellowish batter and text Selena: *Pink is a state of mind.* I'm just relieved that the strawberries were ripe in time, as otherwise I would have tried to do it all with beet juice, and the mixture of beet juice with the bright yellow butter that comes from the local dairy in springtime would probably have made the frosting look very Pepto-Bismol-y.

Of course, those who know the slightest bit of anything about baking already know that my plan to turn the cake pink by simply adding strawberry mush is doomed to produce an over-liquified batter which will bake into a rock-hard (if still marginally edible) slab. The cream cheese/buttercream frosting fares better, taking to the strawberries with style, and at least adding one element to the cake which people can enjoy. And thank god I have also made truly pink ice cream by soaking leftover candy canes that my sister mailed us last Christmas in the milk (okay, yes, I am aware that this is the same red dye I am claiming to be avoiding, but it's *recycled* red dye, and I didn't buy it myself).

Still, edible or not, the cake is beautiful. With the full wisdom and power of her three years, Bright Eyes collects a basketful of flowers from the garden and covers the whole top with big yellow and pink rose blooms and tiny stars of violet borage. The Pragmatist has gone to the non-natural food grocery and infiltrated the house with bright pink non-beeswax birthday candles, thrilling her daughter's pink birthday heart.

So here, below the wide grin of a newly minted "big giwl," is an all-natural pink cake with bright drugstore candles, beside a bowl of organic-milk-plus-corn-syrup-candy ice cream, our mixture of effort and idealism, compromise and caving in. Here she stands on her chair, ready to blow out her candles, and once again I am struck by her innate life-force, as well as her vulnerability. All those tiny eggs, and all my tiny efforts may not save them, or, just as likely, perhaps they will survive and bring her a daughter as lovely and willful as she herself is. I must act without knowing what the result will be. So for today, I offer her this imperfect cake, this imperfect world, the best I have. "Happy Birthday, Bright Eyes. Make a wish."

epilogue

The web that holds our world together is tattered, with all our hopes and dreams suspended in it.

Nina Simons
"From Mourning into Daybreak"

Remember that free pony? (I'd almost forgotten.) Freckles. His ancient, dysfunctional teeth were starving him to death when we got him, but we managed to revive him with twice-a-day slurpable feedings of alfalfa/grain gruel. Once Freckles started to feel better, he stopped acting like the docile, pet-like pony which had been described to us, and more like a regular, butthead pony. But he was close enough to the ground that even his occasional rebellions that sent the toddler perched on his back flying didn't really cause any harm. The boys loved being led around and around the acre clutching onto the saddle with their chubby fingers, daredevils enough not to be scared off by the intermittent falls.

Freckles was never very fast, but he began slowing down significantly by the time Bright Eyes was born and this book began. As Bright Eyes grew, Freckles limped more and more, we rode less and less, and being a hospice nurse, I dispensed his painkillers liberally, aware of the potential for liver damage but more interested in his quality of life than his potential for longevity. He was old already, and I wanted him to be comfortable. So the day he didn't bother to come up for his food—his chief pleasure in life (if you can measure that by the fact that he got an erection every time I filled his bucket)—I called the vet. I explained to the kids that Freckles was hurting, and that the vet was coming, and if she couldn't make him feel better, then she would help him die so he wouldn't have to be in pain.

"Can we cut Freckles' tail off?" Mowgli immediately asked.

"Um, no," I stammered, tripped up by this unexpected request. It seemed almost obscene, callous. "Freckles might want his tail to swat away the flies while we wait for the vet to come."

"Well, if he dies, can we cut it off?"

"Um, well, let me think about that," I deferred. We went on about our morning, bringing Freckles his last meal out to where he was standing unmoving, then having our own breakfast. It seemed mostly like a normal day.

"Mom," Mowgli piped up an hour or so later. "If Freckles dies, can we cut off his feet?"

"Um, uh… his *feet?*"

"Yeah. We could make bowls out of them and use them and always remember him."

"Um, well, I think it would be really messy to cut off his feet, so I don't think I want to do that."

"Oh. Okay." Time for Legos, off he went.

Later in the morning, we went down to check on the pony. Mowgli regarded him with a thoughtful tilt of his head. "Mom, can we eat Freckles?"

He had pretty much rendered me speechless at this point, but I made an effortful recovery: "If we were really hungry, and didn't have enough food to eat or money to buy more, then we would probably eat Freckles. But we have plenty of food, and Freckles wouldn't taste very good, so we are not going to eat him." I willed him not to ask what *was* going to happen to the body once the knacker man came to haul him away, and he didn't. So we just waited for the vet to arrive, and I tried to reconcile my sweet son's loving heart with the fact that he so pragmatically suggested first dismembering, and then eating, our pet.

And then I got it. My son was not a budding psychopath; rather, he was exactly what is needed to save the world: a total ecologist. He was just verbalizing the values I'd been trying, in my half-assed way, to teach him: reduce, reuse, recycle. The new "three Rs" of basic education for a sustainable world. It's not that he didn't care about the ornery Freckles, it's just that he was able to envision a continued usefulness for him beyond the traditional pony-rides. Mowgli, in his own way, would have perpetuated Freckles by transmuting him into a decorative whip of tailhair, four lopsided breakfast dishes, and a number of nourishing meals. He was way ahead of me, which is where his generation will need to be to create a new world in which they can thrive.

Inspired, I tried to figure out how to honor this vision without crossing my personal boundary of "too yucky." Presumably the knacker man would be using Freckles' leftovers in some way, though I wasn't sure I wanted to ask how. I briefly considered renting a backhoe and burying him myself so we could have a family discussion about how Freckles was nourishing our land, but I wasn't so sure it was legal to bury livestock in my neighborhood, or that I could really manage a backhoe with Bright Eyes tagging along. By the time the vet was able to make it over, the boys had gone off for a long-planned playdate, so Mowgli missed seeing Freckles slump slowly to the ground and grow still. And he also missed the vet's unexpected question after she ascertained that there was no heartbeat: "Do you want me to cut off his tail?"

(Clearly outvoted, I aquiesced, dividing the tail into two long elastic-bound literal ponytails for the boys to do with what they will—whip each other, apparently, then decorate their room. Eventually they ended up back outside, forgotten, and for a few seasons now, all the bird's nests I find are threaded through with long white hairs.)

Oh, my astonishing children. Wildness and vision wrapped up all together with practicality and no sense yet of limits to their future. My budding total ecologist may well lead the way to a new way of living here on earth. Meanwhile, I do my best not to squelch his natural optimism while I continue to debate how to inch forward. Currently, I'm pondering technology, and my resistance to it, spurred on, of course, by my current transportation methods (well, what else is new?).

Shortly after Bright Eyes turned a tickled-pink three and my story officially ended, I purchased two previously impossible items: a Prius and a horse. The Prius is semi-justifiable based on my job driving and the fact that by now two out of three children are no longer required to use carseats, so I can go everywhere in the Prius unless (as is often the case) there are extra kids along. (The minivan still hangs around, allowing for playdates, field trip driving, and occasional carpools.) The horse is theoretically justifiable as she is theoretically "for the kids," although if I'm honest, she's here making our tiny "pasture" into a mudlot because she was cheap, and I fell in love with her the moment I saw her.

This dual horse/hybrid acquisition has done a lot to put my former Prius envy into perspective. Of course I love the car, with its integrated phone and GPS (both very helpful to someone who drives around to random houses all night long while answering a pager) and its computer screen constantly broadcasting my righteous fuel savings. And the kids love the screen, too, the closest thing we have to a TV. But getting the horse at the same time highlighted the dangers of all this seductive technology. For one thing, unlike the car, the horse is completely biodegradable. And yes, she does currently eat hay that was harvested with a petroleum-fueled tractor, but unlike the car, she could survive in a post-carbon world. The horse is an incredibly complicated piece of machinery, but unlike the car, she has a capacity for self-healing: the scratch on her side disappears after a few weeks. And she has very few electrical components, of the type that are susceptible to breaking. The Prius is a huge step forward, but it begs the question if forward is the way we should be stepping. Mowgli summed it up when, no longer quite so in thrall to the newness of the Prius, he waxed enthusiastic about the old Civic: "You know what was super-cool about the old car? You could roll down the windows when it wasn't turned on!"

"Yeah!" The Percussionist echoed, "That was *so* awesome." It does make you think about whether technological advances really are more advanced, or just more complicated. Of course, within a week of buying the new (to me) car, I was warned by a friend that the interaction between the electric motor in the front and the battery in the back (or maybe it's the other way around—if I didn't understand the old car, no way I'm going to understand this one) creates an especially strong electromagnetic field in the car itself which is probably unhealthy. I filed this information away with the "always roll down your window when using your cell phone in the car to let the radiation waves escape" folder of possibly true and/ or useful information that I'd rather not deal with just now. What I am sure of, is that when the Prius dies, it will leave more behind than the horse, in terms of stuff, and in terms of environmental impact.

For now, both the current horse and the current Prius are in fine working order. They serve as tangible avatars of two distinct possible pathways forward: back to basics, or what seems like our best bet given how reluctant we all are to give up our creature comforts: better living through green technology. But driving the Prius with all of its circuits and features, automatic everything, keeps me feeling like the technological solution will keep us balancing on a precarious edge.

Six months after I bought the Prius, I totaled it. In another car, the accident might have been a few hundred dollars of body work and a few minor adjustments internally, but the tow guy summed it up as he hoisted my car onto his pulley: "These cars are so complicated, it's easier just to junk them than to fix them." The Prius' features: the smart airbag, the seatbelt pretensioner, the crumple zones, and probably other complicated stuff that I don't know is there, did a great job of protecting my individual bodily integrity. I walked away unscratched. But that first Prius ended up wherever dead hybrids go: hopefully to some very conscientious auto recycler. And with my insurance check, I had to decide what to do next. But since I haven't yet figured out how to leave it all behind: the job, the baseball practice, etc, I bought another one. A few (okay, several) hours on the internet convinced me that the 100% electric car with sufficient range for my job wasn't quite here yet, so for that precise historical moment, for my particular state of consciousness, it was the best available option. And my best is all I can ever do.

Since I wrote this book, my children have grown older and more independent, and as a result I am starting to broaden my perspective. I remain enrolled, by necessity, in the Sally Lee School of Incremental Change, but now I am envisioning an end result a bit more encompassing than just an unblocked drainage ditch or a quart of frozen blackberries. The larger picture of how I want to create my own community, sustainability, and of course, my permaculture garden, comes slowly more and more into focus, now that my easy excuses are playing on their own. And it turns out I'm planting my fruit trees one by one, a foot-high spindly pomegranate replacing a dying decorative bush, a slow removal of invasive stalky weeds to make room for the orange tree I'll buy myself for my birthday this year.

My kids' growth is not the only thing that has happened since I started writing this book. I can now buy shampoo in truly recyclable aluminum bottles, rather than the plastic ones which can only be "downcycled." (Recycling primer: an aluminum bottle can turn into another aluminum bottle, but a plastic bottle can only turn into something less valuable.) LED light bulbs have gotten a lot cheaper. But when I got home after buying one at the hardware store last month, I actually read the fine print on the package, and discovered that the newly affordable "better than compact florescent" bulb might interfere with the function of my cordless phone (which, yes, I am going to finally replace, really, really soon). Which means...

what? The light bulb is sending out its own frequency into the electromagnetic mush of my home created by my existing wiring, phone, and the neighbor's wireless signal? Yikes.

So a lot hasn't changed as well. The icebergs are still melting. There is still a need for urgent political action, and still a need for broader adoption of individual and collective conservation and restoration. On the smallest daily level, I still act out my commitments and my failures, but slowly I can see the balance shifting. For I find that I have changed and continue to do so. Ninety percent of the time, I now use loose tea that I bring home from the teahouse in my refillable tin tea boxes. And those times when I fail to do so, I'm using a brand of tea bags, packaged in pretty take-me-home boxes, but without individual wrappers, strings, staples, or tags, reducing their total waste by a (relative to the size of a teabag) large percentage.

The other day, Selena left her travel mug in my new car by accident, a tea bag tag dangling from the string snaking out from under the lid. After the mug knocked about on the floor of the backseat for a few days, I opened the back door to discover the tag had fallen off and lodged under the edge of the floormat. The car is still shiny-new enough for me to care about these things, so I fished it out to put it in the recycle bin. That particular tea bag tag never made it to the bin, though. It's taped up on my bathroom mirror, to remind me when I forget. On it are printed the words: "Your choices will change the world."

Want to make a change in the world?
Visit www.milliontinythings.com for links to
recommended books and websites.

Acknowledgments

Thanks to the owners and staff, past and present, of Infusions Teahouse, Aqus, Della Fattoria, and all the other cafes where I hung out endlessly re-steeping my tea leaves while I wrote and wrote and rewrote.

My biggest thanks go to two amazing women: my writing teacher and mentor Laurie Wagner midwifed this book into being, and my editor-to-die-for C.A. Carlson ushered it through its adolescence. My gratitude to them knows no bounds.

Without Charity Kirk's amazing eye and astute web advice, this book would not be nearly so pretty, nor would anyone ever find my website. And without Jessica Lee, there would be a million tiny typos.

Thanks to all my friends who read my essays and early drafts and kept encouraging me: Susan, Selena, Lydia, Colleen, Kit, and Kaitlin. And to Lisa and Stephanie, who didn't have time to read the drafts but encouraged me anyway.

Deep gratitude to the groups of women who have helped hold me and this book: the incredible community of Ariel

Gore's School for Wayward Writers, my fabulous if ever-shifting book club, and my schmatta sisters.

Thanks to my mother Sally Lee for inspiring the Sally Lee School of Incremental Bookwriting. And to the rest of my family for, well, being my family. In a good way.

Hearty and heart-felt love to all my wonderful colleagues at Hospice of Petaluma for making life good. That includes you, Sue, even though you left.

Thanks to Watta for her faith in my ability to start a new chapter. And to Molly Stern, who didn't even know me, for offering a stranger some impeccably timed advice and enthusiasm.

Also deserving of thanks: my not-yet-mentioned friends who let themselves be characters--Molly, Lotus, Shannon, Carey and Kate.

And many, many thanks to Irene for holding my hand tightly through the scary process of putting it all out there.

Oh, and anyone else I forgot. I'm sure I forgot lots of people. Like, I almost forgot Arno, who entertained the kids for so many hours (sorry, Arno). If I forgot you, write in your name here _____. You are officially thanked.

And of course, thanks and love to my children – R, T, Z, and C – for the limitless inspiration.

About the Author

Full-time nurse, part-time environmentalist, and all-the-time mother, Kenna Lee lives in Sebastopol, California, with her three semi-feral children and several domesticated animals. She can be reached through www.milliontinythings.com.